How to use your Snap Rev___ ____ ___

This 'Frankenstein' Snap Revision Text Guide will ___
English Literature exam. It is divided into two-pa___
help for the bits you find tricky. This book cover___
the exam:

Plot: what happens in the novel?

Setting and Context: what periods, places, events and attitudes are relevant to understanding the novel?

Characters: who are the main characters, how are they presented, and how do they change?

Themes: what ideas does the author explore in the novel, and how are they shown?

The Exam: what kinds of question will come up in your exam, and how can you get top marks?

To help you get ready for your exam, each two-page topic includes the following:

Key Quotations to Learn

Short quotations to memorise that will allow you to analyse in the exam and boost your grade.

Summary

A recap of the most important points covered in the topic.

Sample Analysis

An example of the kind of analysis that the examiner will be looking for.

Quick Test

A quick-fire test to check you can remember the main points from the topic.

Exam Practice

A short writing task so you can practise applying what you've covered in the topic.

Glossary

A handy list of words you will find useful when revising 'Frankenstein' with easy-to-understand definitions.

AUTHOR: RACHEL GRANT

ebook

To access the ebook version of this Snap Revision Text Guide, visit

collins.co.uk/ebooks

and follow the step-by-step instructions.

Published by Collins
An imprint of HarperCollins*Publishers*
1 London Bridge Street
London SE1 9GF

© HarperCollins*Publishers* Limited 2017

ISBN 9780008247126

First published 2017

10 9 8 7 6 5 4 3

All rights reserved. No part of this publication
may be reproduced, stored in a retrieval
system, or transmitted, in any form or by any
means, electronic, mechanical, photocopying,
recording or otherwise, without the prior
permission of Collins.

British Library Cataloguing in Publication Data.

A CIP record of this book is available from the
British Library.

Printed in the UK by Martins the Printer Ltd.

Commissioning Editor: Gillian Bowman
Managing Editor: Craig Balfour
Author: Rachel Grant
Copyeditor: David Christie
Proofreaders: Jill Laidlaw and Louise Robb
Project management and typesetting:
  Mark Steward
Cover designers: Kneath Associates and
  Sarah Duxbury
Production: Natalia Rebow

ACKNOWLEDGEMENTS

The author and publisher are grateful to
the copyright holders for permission to use
quoted materials and images.

Every effort has been made to trace copyright
holders and obtain their permission for the
use of copyright material. The author and
publisher will gladly receive information
enabling them to rectify any error or omission
in subsequent editions. All facts are correct at
time of going to press.

MIX
Paper from
responsible source

FSC
www.fsc.org
FSC® C007454

This book is produced from independently
certified FSC™ paper to ensure responsible
forest management.

For more information visit:
www.harpercollins.co.uk/green

Contents

Walton's Letters I to IV

You must be able to: understand what happens at the beginning of the novel.

What do we learn from the Preface?

The **preface** is by the poet Percy Bysshe Shelley, who was Mary Shelley's husband. It describes the origin of the story. A group of friends were travelling near Geneva in the summer of 1816 and to amuse themselves during the cold and rainy evenings, they told each other ghost stories.

What is the setting?

Captain Robert Walton writes to his sister Margaret from St Petersburg at the start of his expedition to the North Pole. Letters I to III focus on his motivation for undertaking the expedition. He is a loner and has no close friends, also, he's looking for adventure. Although the trip will be dangerous, he is hoping it will give him a life purpose and some sort of glory.

In Letter IV, some 8 months after Letter I, he writes that his ship has got stuck in ice in the far north.

While waiting for the ice to break, Walton sees a sledge with a gigantic figure being pulled by dogs in the distance.

What do we learn about the stranger?

A piece of ice brings a stranger to the ship. He is half-dead and exhausted. As Walton nurses him back to health, he gets to know and admire the stranger. They develop a friendly relationship. The stranger decides to tell Walton his life story. He hopes that Walton will learn a lesson from it.

The stranger recognises something of himself in Walton. Walton's curiosity and excitement about hearing the stranger's narrative sets up the reader for what follows. His story will be marvellous, strange and harrowing.

Key Quotations to Learn

I desire the company of a man who could sympathise with me; (Walton: Letter II)

... a being which had the shape of a man, but apparently of gigantic stature, (Walton: Letter IV)

Strange and harrowing must be his story, (Walton: Letter IV)

Summary

- Walton gets ready for his expedition, starting at St Petersburg.
- At the start, he is in good spirits and all goes well.
- While marooned in ice, Walton sees a huge figure on a sledge go past in the distance.
- Walton befriends a different stranger who will tell his life story.

Questions

QUICK TEST
1. Where does Walton begin his voyage?
2. Who is Walton writing to?
3. What does Walton see before he meets the stranger?
4. How does Walton help the stranger?
5. Why does the stranger decide to tell Walton his life story?

EXAM PRACTICE
Using one or more of the 'Key Quotations to Learn', write a paragraph explaining how Shelley prepares the reader for the stranger's narrative.

Chapters 1 to 4

You must be able to: understand what happens in Chapters 1 to 4.

What is the stranger's background?

He was born and brought up in Geneva and he is the eldest of three children. His sister, Elizabeth, is an orphan, adopted by the stranger's parents. His younger brother is named William.

We learn that the stranger's name is Victor Frankenstein and that he had an extremely happy childhood and a loving family. He had one very close friend, Henry Clerval, a merchant's son.

Henry is portrayed as very different in character to Victor, being artistic and romantic in temperament. Victor's interests lie in science and mathematics.

What things change the course of Victor's life?

At 15, Victor witnesses an electrical storm, which makes him fascinated by electricity and **galvanism**.

When he is 17, his beloved mother dies from scarlet fever. Her dying wish is that Victor and Elizabeth should at some point marry.

Although grief-stricken, Victor decides to go to Ingolstadt University to study science. He leaves his family and Clerval behind.

Why does Victor want to create new life?

Victor is very ambitious and he gets carried away with his studies. He works hard but has an inflated sense of his own power. He senses he is being driven by fate, which is more powerful than himself – yet his own ego also drives him on. Once he has discovered the secret of creating life, he is determined to 'father' a new species.

Intending to bring a being to life, Victor collects body parts from graves and charnel houses (buildings where dead bodies are kept). He does this in secret, after dark, as he knows it is a shameful activity. In doing this, he cuts himself off from his family and friends.

Key Quotations to Learn

Destiny was too potent, (Victor: Chapter 2)

... I succeeded in discovering the cause of generation and life; (Victor: Chapter 4)

... I pursued nature to her hiding places. (Victor: Chapter 4)

Summary

- Victor's home and family life is blissful.
- His mother dies when he is 17.
- Victor leaves home to study science at university.
- Victor is driven by his ambition to discover how to create new life.
- He becomes isolated from friends and family.

Questions

QUICK TEST
1. What are the names of Victor's sister and brother?
2. Who is Victor's best friend?
3. What important events happen when he is 17?
4. What is the driving force of Victor's ambition?
5. Why does Victor visit graves and charnel houses at night?

EXAM PRACTICE
Using one or more of the 'Key Quotations to Learn', write a paragraph explaining why Victor is driven to create new life.

Chapters 5 to 8

You must be able to: understand what happens in Chapters 5 to 8.

How does Frankenstein react to the Creature?

As soon as the Creature draws breath, Victor knows he has made a terrible mistake. He's utterly horrified and repulsed by the Creature's hideous appearance. He's appalled that all his hard work has resulted in something so horrible.

He goes to sleep, exhausted, and then, when the Creature wakes him up, he runs away and hides. In fact, he utterly rejects the thing he has created, or 'fathered'.

What happens to the Creature?

When Victor returns to his workshop, the Creature has disappeared. We hear nothing more of him directly until much later, but we sense that the Creature is always on Victor's mind from this moment on. Recalling that night and the monster he created actually makes Victor ill.

Is Victor's life back to normal?

His friend Henry brings news from home and he helps Victor to recover from his illness. It takes two years, but with the help of his friend and family, Victor's happy frame of mind seems restored.

The shocking news of his brother William's murder spurs Victor to return home. On the way, he witnesses another electrical storm and in the darkness, he has a glimpse of the Creature.

Who is Justine Moritz?

Justine Moritz is a trusted servant of the Frankenstein family who had recently returned to the house. A locket containing a picture of Victor's mother is found in Justine's pocket and this is taken as proof that she murdered William. There is nothing Elizabeth or Victor can do to help Justine, especially when Justine decides to confess to a crime she did not commit.

The unfairness of the situation, and his own suspicion that it was the Creature that killed William, together throw Victor into another fit of guilty depression. Elizabeth tries to comfort him, but this time his family seem powerless to help him.

Key Quotations to Learn

Oh! no mortal could support the horror of that countenance! (Victor: Chapter 5)

The form of the monster on whom I had bestowed existence was for ever before my eyes, (Victor: Chapter 5)

... dreams that had been my food and pleasant rest ... were now become a hell to me; (Victor: Chapter 5)

Summary

- Victor succeeds in creating life but is appalled and horrified by the Creature's appearance.
- In shock, Victor falls ill but, with Henry's help, recovers.
- Meanwhile the Creature has disappeared.
- Learning that his brother William has been murdered, Victor returns home.
- Justine Moritz is accused of the murder.
- The Frankenstein family do their best to defend Justine.
- Although she is innocent, Justine decides to confess – and is hanged.

Questions

QUICK TEST
1. Why does Victor reject the Creature?
2. Why does Victor fall ill?
3. What happens to William?
4. How much time passes between the birth of the Creature and Victor's next sighting of him?
5. Why does Victor feel guilty when Justine is executed?

EXAM PRACTICE
Using one or more of the 'Key Quotations to Learn', write a paragraph explaining the effect that the birth of the Creature has on Victor.

Chapters 9 to 12

You must be able to: understand what happens in Chapters 9 to 12.

Where do Victor and the Creature meet?

After Justine is hanged, Victor decides to travel to the Alps. He visits places he knew as a boy and the immensity and grandeur of the mountains helps him to feel better. He responds to the icy vista of the Alps as a **Romantic** poet would, calling them '**sublime**'.

Here the Creature finds Victor. We have a physical description of his stature (he is bigger than a human) and superhuman speed, and learn that the Creature is miserable and wretched.

At first, Victor rejects the Creature but then he reluctantly agrees to listen to his story.

What is the Creature's story?

Soon after fleeing the scene of his own creation, the Creature tries to approach some villagers, but they are terrified and attack him. This makes him realise he can never be part of society. Finding a hovel, he takes refuge from the wintry cold.

A family lives in the cottage next door and, although he keeps himself hidden, the Creature observes them. This teaches him about human emotions, family love and relationships. He yearns to belong to a family such as this.

However, when he catches sight of his own reflection in a pool, he realises how hideous he looks. This makes him depressed and ashamed.

We learn that he is desperately lonely, sensitive and highly intelligent.

What attracts the Creature to the cottagers?

The Creature's sensitivity is shown in the way he describes his impressions of the natural world. As he observes the cottagers he becomes entranced by their beauty, gentleness, kindness and the affection they show to each other.

Family love and human affection are what the Creature craves – and that is why he decides to make himself known to the family. He is sure they will not reject him.

Key Quotations to Learn

Abhorred monster! Fiend that thou art! (Victor: Chapter 10)

It was indeed a paradise compared to the bleak forest, (The Creature: Chapter 11)

I looked upon them as superior beings ... (The Creature: Chapter 12)

Summary

- Victor travels to the Alps, alone.
- The Creature finds Victor in an isolated and icy spot.
- The Creature tells how he is shunned by humans and society.
- He finds a hovel to live in, next to a cottage.
- He secretly observes the family who lives there.
- Over time, the Creature grows to love the family and decides to approach them.

Questions

QUICK TEST
1. Why does Victor decide to travel to the Alps?
2. What happened when the Creature approached humans?
3. How did the Creature find out he is hideous to look at?
4. What did the Creature observe in the cottagers?
5. What does the Creature long for, more than anything else?

EXAM PRACTICE
Using one or more of the 'Key Quotations to Learn', write a paragraph describing what we have learned about the Creature's qualities at this point in the novel.

Chapters 13 to 16

You must be able to: understand what happens in Chapters 13 to 16.

Who arrives at the cottage?

A mysterious stranger called Safie arrives at the cottage. She is from Arabia, and as she learns the cottagers' language, the Creature learns with her.

The creature learns that the cottagers are a family called De Lacey. The son is Felix and the daughter Agatha, and they are of noble birth but were expelled from their home in France.

What is Safie's story?

Safie's father, a Turk, was falsely accused of a crime and sent to prison. Felix fell in love with Safie and wished to marry her. He helped Safie's father to escape and gain safe passage from Paris. However, the plot was discovered. Old De Lacey, Felix and Agatha were imprisoned.

Safie's father then betrayed Felix, telling his daughter that she could never marry Felix. He commanded her to join him in Constantinople. Safie secretly escaped to join the De Laceys, now exiled from France and living in Germany.

What happens to the Creature?

After a long time, the Creature decides to approach old, blind De Lacey. Because he is blind, De Lacey speaks openly to the Creature but when the others arrive, they are horrified. Felix attacks him, and the Creature flees.

How does the Creature feel?

For the Creature, this is another bitter reminder that he can never be part of a family or human society. At length, he returns to the cottage but the De Laceys are leaving, in fear of their lives. In a rage of anger and misery, the Creature burns down the cottage.

From this point on, the Creature decides he will turn from 'good' to 'evil', as all his attempts to be accepted have been spurned. In this mindset and swearing revenge on Frankenstein, he murders William and then frames Justine for the murder.

Now the Creature is so lonely he begs Victor to make him a mate – a female Creature that is as deformed and horrible as himself. If Victor does this, the Creature promises he will disappear from Victor's life forever.

Key Quotations to Learn

'Accursed creator! Why did you form a monster so hideous that even you turned from me in disgust?' (The Creature: Chapter 15)

'Cursed, cursed Creator! Why did I live?' (The Creature: Chapter 16)

Summary

- Safie arrives at the cottage and the Creature learns language and educates himself.
- The Creature learns Safie's story.
- Now sure that the De Laceys will help him, the Creature approaches old De Lacey for help.
- The family reject the Creature and, in a rage, he burns down their cottage.
- The Creature vows revenge on Victor, murders William and frames Justine.
- The Creature begs Victor to make him a mate.

Questions

QUICK TEST
1. What is the family name of the cottagers?
2. How does the Creature learn to read and speak?
3. How did Safie get to the cottage?
4. What did the Creature do when the cottagers left?
5. What strange request does the Creature have for Victor?

EXAM PRACTICE
Using one of the 'Key Quotations to Learn', write a paragraph explaining why the Creature wanted revenge on Victor.

You must be able to: understand what happens in Chapters 17 to 20.

Why does Victor agree to make the Creature a mate?

Though appalled by the idea, Victor agrees to the Creature's request. We are told that Victor feels it is his responsibility to offer his creation some sort of happiness. Fear also plays a part: Victor knows what the Creature is capable of and wants him out of his life forever.

Why does Victor delay?

Victor finds excuse after excuse to put off fulfilling his side of the bargain. The truth is he really does not want to make the creature a mate.

In promising to marry Elizabeth when he gets back from England, Victor makes a bargain with himself. Once he completes his task, he will be free to marry and live a normal life again. However, we know that Victor's life has not been normal since he brought the Creature to life – so how can two wrongs make a right?

What is different about this 'birth'?

Compared to when he made the Creature, Victor's state of mind in the Orkney Islands could not be more different. Victor is no longer full of ambition and dreams of glory; he is wretched and miserable. His laboratory in Orkney is a broken-down hut. He dreads what he must do.

Why does Victor destroy the She-Creature?

One night, as Victor thinks about the effects his action might have on the future of the human race, he sees the Creature's hideous face staring through the window. Victor instantly realises the Creature has followed Victor's every step, to make sure that he fulfils his promise.

Overcome with passion, Victor destroys the She-Creature right in front of the Creature. The Creature howls and disappears. After a while, he returns to confront Victor. Now Victor has broken his promise, the Creature vows to take the most terrible vengeance.

Victor stands up to the Creature, but it takes all his strength – and he is terrified by the Creature's threat, 'I shall be with you on your wedding night'.

When Victor lands in Ireland, he is surprised to be greeted with suspicion and hostility just because he is a stranger. A man was murdered the night before and Victor must go to the local magistrate, Mr Kirwin, to explain how and why he has arrived in Ireland.

Key Quotations to Learn

... I felt that there was some justice in his argument. (Victor: Chapter 17)

It was, indeed, a filthy process in which I was engaged. During my first experiment a kind of enthusiastic frenzy had blinded me to the horror of my employment; (Victor: Chapter 19)

'I shall be with you on your wedding night.' (The Creature: Chapter 20)

Summary

- Victor agrees to make a mate for the Creature.
- With Henry, Victor travels to England to gather information.
- Before he goes, Victor asks Elizabeth to marry him and to wait for his return.
- As he gets ready to create the She-Creature, he sees the Creature staring at him through the window. In a fit of passion, Victor destroys the She-Creature.
- Intending to dump the body in the sea, Victor is blown off course.
- When he comes ashore in Ireland, Victor is suspected of murder.

Questions

QUICK TEST
1. Why does Victor delay making the She-Creature?
2. Where does Victor go to create the She-Creature?
3. Why does he destroy it?
4. What threat does the Creature issue to Victor?
5. What happens to Victor when he arrives in Ireland?

EXAM PRACTICE
Using one or more of the 'Key Quotations to Learn', write a paragraph explaining why Victor at first agreed but then refused to do what the Creature asked.

Chapters 21 to 24

You must be able to: understand what happens in Chapters 21 to 24.

Who is the murdered man?

We learn that the man was strangled, with black finger marks visible on his neck. This tells Victor that it was the Creature who committed the crime. However, Victor is unprepared for the shock that follows: the murdered man is his old friend, Henry Clerval.

Victor falls into a fever and during this time he raves about his own guilt for the deaths of Justine, William and Henry. When he comes around, Victor is accused of the murder. Luckily, Mr Kirwin, the magistrate, sends for Victor's father and at the trial Kirwin proves that Victor is innocent. Although he is a free man, Victor remains tortured by his past.

Why is Victor nervous about his wedding day?

Victor cannot forget the Creature's threat, 'I shall be with you on your wedding night'. He sees this as a threat to his own life, but by this point in the story we suspect that Elizabeth is in greater danger. Victor does not tell Elizabeth anything before they are married. Instead, he gets increasingly nervous, aware that the Creature is certainly watching Victor's every move.

How are we told of Elizabeth's death?

The text passage that leads up to Elizabeth's murder is full of tension. Victor is terrified; he carries a pistol and sends Elizabeth to bed while he patrols the dark corners. Suddenly he hears a scream – too late, he realises that the Creature has attacked his wife. He finds her lifeless body lying across the bed.

How does Victor react to this tragedy?

First, Victor faints with grief and then, seeing the Creature at the window, shoots at him – but misses. He feels utterly without hope, horrified at what he has done, and also cursed and doomed.

When his father, in grief, dies a few days later, Victor decides to confess everything to a magistrate. **Ironically**, the magistrate does not believe him. It seems to Victor that his only course of action is to pursue and kill the Creature himself – or die in the attempt.

Is the Creature pursuer or pursued?

Victor tracks the creature but it is clear that the Creature has the upper hand. He taunts Victor with messages and Victor endures terrible hardship. He leads Victor through the icy wastes of the North – which is where Victor meets Walton and tells his story.

Key Quotations to Learn

Mine has been a tale of horrors; (Victor: Chapter 23)

I was cursed by some devil and carried about with me my eternal hell; (Victor: Chapter 24)

'My reign is not yet over ...' (The Creature: Chapter 24)

Summary

- Henry Clerval was strangled by the Creature.
- Victor is tried for the crime, but acquitted.
- Victor marries Elizabeth, despite the Creature's threat.
- The Creature murders Elizabeth on her wedding night.
- Victor's father dies of grief.
- Victor confesses everything to a magistrate, but is not believed.
- Victor vows to hunt down the Creature, who leads him on for many months.
- Ill and exhausted, Victor boards Walton's ship.

Questions

QUICK TEST

1. How was Henry Clerval murdered?
2. Who really murdered Henry?
3. What plays on Victor's mind as his wedding day gets closer?
4. What happens when Victor confesses to a magistrate?
5. How does the Creature continue to inflict misery on Victor?

EXAM PRACTICE

Using one or more of the 'Key Quotations to Learn', write a paragraph describing the relationship between Victor and the Creature at this point in the novel.

Walton, in Continuation

You must be able to: understand what happens at the end of the novel.

Does Walton believe Victor's story?

Walton is compelled to believe Victor's incredible story, even while acknowledging it is very strange. Two things convince him of its truth: one – he has actually seen the Creature himself at a distance, across the ice; two – Victor has shown him copies of the letters between Felix and Safie.

Why does Walton decide to turn for home?

The ship has been stuck in ice for more than a week and the crew is disheartened and rebellious. Walton himself is frightened they may not get out alive; therefore, as soon as the ice breaks, he decides to take his chance and turn south.

How does Walton's story end?

Victor intends to continue his pursuit of the Creature, seeing it as his fate and destiny. However, he is still very weak. The effort of trying to leave the ship causes him to faint and he delivers one final speech before he dies. Walton is distraught.

The Creature comes to pay his respects to his creator. Walton finds him weeping over the coffin and his words show remorse for the crimes he has committed. At the same time, he claims the evil he has done was horrible to him, and that he himself suffered far more than Victor, as he was a good being forced by events to turn to evil.

At first, Walton feels sympathy for the Creature but then he remembers what Victor has told him, and he accuses him of **hypocrisy**. In reply, the Creature points out that Walton has heard only Victor's side of the story. He confesses to all his crimes but reminds Walton that his own life was cursed from the start and that despite trying many times to be accepted by society, he was forever an outcast.

His final words show his complicated relationship with Frankenstein: they both lived only to seek revenge on the other and now that Victor is dead, the Creature views his own death as a release.

Key Quotations to Learn

'Seek happiness in tranquillity and avoid ambition ...' (Victor: September 12th)

'Oh Frankenstein! Generous and self-devoted being!' (The Creature: September 12th)

'... the fallen angel becomes a malignant devil.' (The Creature: September 12th)

'... Blasted as thou wert, my agony was still superior to thine ...'
(The Creature: September 12th)

Summary

- Walton writes to his sister that he believes Victor's story.
- The ship's crew persuade Walton to abandon the voyage and return home.
- Trying to leave the ship in his weakened state, Victor dies.
- The Creature visits his corpse and weeps.
- The Creature tells Walton he is sorry for all he has done and that he is ready to die.
- He leaves the ship and disappears into the darkness.

Questions

QUICK TEST
1. What two things convince Walton that Victor has told the truth?
2. Why does Victor want to leave the ship?
3. What is Walton's reaction to Victor's death?
4. How does Walton react to the Creature?
5. What links Victor and the Creature to the very end?

EXAM PRACTICE
Using one or more of the 'Key Quotations to Learn', write a paragraph analysing the Creature's thoughts and feelings at the end of the novel.

Narrative Framing

You must be able to: explain the significance of the different narrative frames Shelley uses to structure the novel.

How did Shelley use framing to draw readers into the novel?

Shelley uses three first-person narratives to tell the story. Walton's letters to Margaret introduce Victor's narrative. The Creature's story starts approximately in the middle (Chapters 11 to 16). A further flashback, Safie's story, comes in Chapter 14, which is in the middle of the Creature's narrative.

This careful construction invites readers to consider the credibility of each narrator. How far do we believe each one? Shelley reminds us at points in the novel that we are reading one person's version of the truth.

Why did Shelley choose to use Walton's letters as the outer framing narrative?

In a sense, Walton is the main narrator, as we rely on him to tell us exactly what Victor says, and we hear what the Creature says as reported by Victor to Walton. Therefore, it is very important that Walton is established as sensible, **rational** and credible. Shelley deliberately chooses Walton to give credibility to the fantastic story he is told.

Walton's sister Margaret is the invisible 'audience' for the whole novel, and this gives a backdrop of normality to the fantastic narratives of Victor and the Creature. It is significant that Walton himself sees and speaks to the Creature at the end – therefore, unless we think Walton is mad or dreaming, the story must have really happened.

Why did Shelley use three first-person narratives to structure the novel?

Shelley used multiple narratives because no single narrator knows the whole story. Therefore, we need to hear from all three narrators in order to understand what happened. Another important effect is that the interlocking narratives create a sense of distance as we move through the novel. We start with the 'real world' of Walton, move through Victor's narrative and by the time we get to the Creature's story, in the middle of the book, it takes on a sense of something far distant, almost mythological in tone. We then return to the real world – the present day – at the end.

Key Quotations to Learn

Remember, I am not recording the vision of a madman. (Victor: Chapter 4)

Even the sailors feel the power of his eloquence: when he speaks they no longer despair; (Walton: September 2nd)

'Hear my tale; it is long and strange ...' (The Creature: Chapter 10)

Summary

- Shelley uses narrative framing of three first-person narratives.
- The structure is symmetrical: the narratives lead into and then out of each other.
- Shelley chooses the rational Walton as the 'outer frame' narrator in order to establish credibility.
- Shelley creates doubt in the reader's mind by having several versions of the same events given by different narrators.
- Shelley's technique forces readers to consider how far they are persuaded by the 'truth' of each narrative.

Questions

QUICK TEST
1. What narrative structure does Shelley use in the novel?
2. What is the function of Walton's narrative in the novel?
3. What is one effect of this narrative technique?
4. Why is it important that Walton speaks to the Creature?

EXAM PRACTICE
Using one or more of the 'Key Quotations to Learn', write a paragraph explaining why Shelley chose to use narrative framing to structure the novel.

The Birth of *Frankenstein*

You must be able to: understand how the novel's meaning was shaped by the writer's life and the time in which she was writing.

Who was Mary Shelley and how did her background influence the novel?

Shelley's father was a political philosopher, William Godwin. Her mother was philosopher and **feminist**, Mary Wollstonecraft. She died soon after giving birth to Mary.

Mary had an unconventional education for a woman at the time. Highly intelligent and very well read, especially about the thinking of the day, she was used to discussing **philosophy** and ideas. All her writing had a strong political theme and *Frankenstein* is no exception. In it, she asks us to consider such questions as what is 'society'? What does it mean for men to be 'equal'? Can man create his own moral order or is it divinely given to man through nature?

How did Mary Shelley's experiences influence the novel?

In 1817, Mary and four friends were on holiday in Switzerland. The friends were her future husband, Percy Bysshe Shelley, Lord Byron, Claire Clairmont and Dr Polidori. Shelley and Byron were both poets and Byron was already famous (or infamous) for his shocking behaviour and **radical** thinking.

Bored and fed up with the rainy weather, the group decided to tell each other ghost stories. Each person had to come up with a story and the group would judge which was scariest.

Mary's contribution was *Frankenstein*, but the story did not come easily, finally, the idea for it came to her in a dream. She was only 19 years old but she was daring, bold and unconventional. *Frankenstein* is a shocking novel now but when it was published it was even more so. It deals with ideas about what happens when man attempts to control nature and oversteps the natural boundaries of humanity. A man 'gives birth' to a monster and the monster destroys him. That Shelley did not flinch from presenting such ideas shows that she was unafraid in considering alternative viewpoints and to step outside the narrow confines of convention. She was open to exploring the radical political and scientific ideas of her day.

Key Quotation to Learn

... this story was begun in the majestic region where the scene is principally laid ... (Preface)

Summary

- Shelley was the daughter of two radical thinkers and had an unconventional education.
- Mary's mother died 11 days after giving birth to her.
- Shelley wrote *Frankenstein* on holiday with two men who were known for their unconventional lifestyles.
- Shelley needed to think of a story shocking and bold enough to hold their attention.
- She had an intellect and background that enabled her to pose radical philosophical, moral and political questions in the novel.

Questions

QUICK TEST
1. What happened to Mary's mother shortly after giving birth?
2. What was unconventional about Mary's education?
3. Where was Mary Shelley when she first thought of the story?
4. What kind of contest did the friends decide to hold?

EXAM PRACTICE
Write a paragraph explaining how Shelley's background and experiences might have influenced the themes and ideas she explores in *Frankenstein*.

The French Revolution

You must be able to: understand the political ideas and context that the writer explored in the novel.

What happened during the French Revolution?

The **French Revolution** was a **populist** uprising inspired by liberal and radical ideas. In 1789, the 'mob' (the ordinary people) furiously stormed the **Bastille** and effectively deposed the French monarch, establishing a **republic**. This event was followed by one of the most violent and bloody periods of European history, the **Reign of Terror**, in which mass executions took place. The political and social effects of this period were far-reaching and it is considered a watershed event that changed Europe forever.

How did it influence thinking at the time *Frankenstein* was written?

The revolution was over by the time Shelley wrote *Frankenstein*, but the horror of its violence and conflict remained fresh in peoples' memories, particularly in northern Europe, where *Frankenstein* is set. The old **hierarchies** of monarchy and gentry continued to be questioned and a new force for democratic representation of the people was in action.

In her portrayal of the Creature, Shelley presents an outsider rejected by society and regarded as inferior for his hideous appearance, despite his intelligence and sensitivity. The Creature is denied access to family, love and community. Knowing he can never belong to society, he decides to turn to evil. Shelley appears to be asking what value there is in a society that prizes appearance over inner worth and passes shallow judgement. She asks us to consider what the consequences might be if society turns its back on individuals.

By creating the Creature, Victor unleashes a powerful force that is super-natural (that is, bigger and more powerful than nature itself). A sort of evil Superman, the Creature cannot be tamed or reasoned with. Having been rejected, he rejects human **morality** and laws and is relentless in his desire for revenge.

This could be interpreted as Shelley's response to the Reign of Terror. The Creature's murderous violence knows no end – he will continue to kill until his own creator, Frankenstein, is dead – much like the mob during the Reign of Terror.

Victor tells Walton that he will be able to draw a 'moral' from his story. Perhaps, one such moral is that revenge and violence, no matter how justified in the mind of the perpetrator, leads only to more violence and solves nothing.

Key Quotation to Learn

... I imagine that you may deduce an apt moral from my tale; (Victor: Letter IV)

Summary

- The French Revolution had a profound effect on thinking in the early part of the nineteenth century.
- Decades later, civilised societies of northern Europe still feared the unleashed violence of the 'mob'.
- In the character of the Creature, Shelley explores various themes linked to the French Revolution and its aftermath.
- The Creature can be viewed as both the rejected outsider from society and the common 'mob' that takes vengeance if mistreated.

Questions

QUICK TEST
1. What was the 'mob'?
2. What was the Reign of Terror?
3. Which character can be linked to the 'mob' of the French Revolution?
4. What is one moral that we might draw from Victor's story as told to Walton?

EXAM PRACTICE
I considered the being whom I had cast among mankind, and endowed with the will and power to effect purposes of horror. (Victor: Chapter 7)

Relating your ideas to the context of the French Revolution, write a paragraph explaining how the Creature could be seen as representative of the 'mob'.

The Romantic Movement

You must be able to: understand how philosophical thinking of the time influenced some ideas that the writer chose to explore in the novel.

What was the Romantic Movement?

The word 'Romantic' in Shelley's time had a different meaning than it does today. Then, it was a name given to a movement – the **Romantic Movement** – that opposed the ideas of the **Enlightenment**, which proposed that man could understand (and even control) the world through science, logic and rational thought.

By contrast, Romantics believed that the world ('Nature') was essentially unknowable and mysterious. They thought that man should not try to control Nature but should be in awe of its 'sublime' power. Romantic poets, such as Percy Bysshe Shelley and Lord Byron, held that feelings and emotions were as important, if not more so, than the knowledge and insight of scientific enquiry that promises control and power over nature, and man.

How does this play out in *Frankenstein*?

Victor's pursuit of knowledge and ambitions for scientific inquiry can be viewed as a moral judgement on Enlightenment thinking. It is against humanity and against nature. What Victor creates is something that contravenes natural law. Remember that Victor raids charnel houses to find body parts – an unnatural act.

At several points in the novel, Victor is uplifted by nature. For example, he is struck by the immensity of Mont Blanc, electric storms and Swiss lakes. The Creature too is moved by the beauty of nature when spring comes. These moments redeem the characters from the unnatural actions they commit at other times. Shelley seems to be saying that nature has the power to make us focus on things greater than ourselves, drawing us out of our own petty concerns. In this way, she is very much a Romantic.

How is the Creature's situation typically 'Romantic'?

Romantics tended to favour the rights of the individual over the collective or state. This idea is explored through the Creature who is presented as a highly sensitive individual, but misunderstood and mistreated by human society. The more he understands and admires human relationships, the more bitter and miserable he becomes, knowing that these experiences are forever denied to him.

Key Quotations to Learn

... I will pioneer a new way, explore unknown powers, and unfold to the world the deepest mysteries of creation. (Victor: Chapter 3)

'Happy, happy earth! Fit habitation for gods,' (The Creature: Chapter 12)

'... I am solitary and abhorred.' (The Creature: Chapter 15)

Summary

- The Romantics believed that although science might bring understanding, man should not aim to know all things.
- Victor and the Creature share a love of nature and are sensitive to its beauty and power.
- Victor's pursuit of knowledge results in an unnatural and monstrous creation.
- The Creature rejects human society as it has rejected him; appreciation of it brings him only misery.

Questions

QUICK TEST
1. What ideas did the Romantic Movement oppose?
2. How did the Romantics view Nature?
3. In what way is Victor an example of Enlightenment thinking?
4. In what way is he an example of Romantic thinking?

EXAM PRACTICE
Using one or more of the 'Key Quotations to Learn', write a paragraph on how the ideas of the Romantic Movement influenced Shelley's characterisation in *Frankenstein*.

Gothic Fiction

You must be able to: understand how the literary context influenced the writing of the novel.

In what ways is *Frankenstein* a Gothic novel?

Gothic fiction became popular in the late eighteenth century. Its purpose was to entertain readers by exciting their emotions and feelings. It often dealt with **supernatural** happenings and told strange stories intended to inspire terror, sometimes horror, and to thrill its readers. It was popular with and marketed to female readers.

Gothic fiction was one example of a fashionable fascination with strange occurrences that defied rational explanation. *Frankenstein* fulfils many of the criteria of a Gothic novel. It is a strange story that defies rational explanation. Recall that the challenge for Shelley was to write a ghost story intended to terrify and enthral her listeners.

What Gothic elements does Mary Shelley include?

The story contains things that are unnatural and uncivilised – the Creature is an outsider and is described as bigger than a man, superhuman in power and unnaturally hideous.

Shelley chooses wild and isolated spots as key plot locations. Victor and the Creature meet on a snowy mountainside; Walton and Victor meet on an ice-locked ship; Victor sees the Creature in the middle of a stormy night. Placing people in dark and isolated places is a theme of Gothic fiction. Victor's laboratory is isolated and dark. The creature comes to life on 'a dreary night of November' and the She-Creature is destroyed at night in an isolated hut in Orkney.

Gothic fiction has an obsession with death, corpses and dark places; Victor visits charnel houses at night to source body parts and then he literally raises them from the dead when he gives life to the Creature.

Gothic fiction has dark passageways, creaking doors and stairways, shadows and unexplained screams of terror. When Victor is on patrol in the dark passageways with a pistol, ready to defend himself against the lurking Creature whom he knows is near, he hears a scream and, too late, discovers Elizabeth's murdered corpse. Violent death is another theme of Gothic fiction. In *Frankenstein*, William, Elizabeth and Henry are murdered and Justine is hanged.

Gothic fiction thrives on creating fear in readers and one of the ways it does this is to build suspense by having the reader know more than the characters. We can see this in *Frankenstein* when Victor attempts to restore normality to his life. Readers sense that his life can never be normal again and that the Creature is following him closely, ready to strike again. In Gothic fiction, characters have uneasy, vague fears of what is not known. Shelley uses the Creature to create a constant sense of unease in the reader's mind.

Key Quotations to Learn

... I thought that I held the corpse of my dead mother in my arms; (Victor: Chapter 5)

I started from my sleep with horror ... (Victor: Chapter 5)

... her bloodless arms and relaxed form flung by the murderer on its bridal bier. (Victor: Chapter 23)

Summary

- *Frankenstein* belongs in the tradition of Gothic fiction.
- Gothic fiction was popular with and marketed to women readers and was intended to thrill and shock.
- It dealt with strange, unnatural happenings that defied rational explanation.
- Shelley intended to write a ghost story to terrify and enthral listeners.

Questions

QUICK TEST
1. What was the purpose of Gothic fiction?
2. Which readers were drawn to Gothic fiction?
3. In what way does the purpose of *Frankenstein* make it a Gothic novel?

EXAM PRACTICE
Relating your ideas to the context of Gothic fiction, write a paragraph showing how Shelley uses Gothic elements in the novel.

Paradise Lost

You must be able to: analyse how Shelley uses ideas from creation stories in the novel.

As well as the **Prometheus myth**, ideas and language from another **creation story** feature heavily in the novel – *Paradise Lost*, an **epic poem** by John Milton.

What is the story in *Paradise Lost*?

Paradise Lost tells the **Biblical** story of the creation and the fall of the first humans, Adam and Eve. It also tells how the archangel Satan was punished for his vanity and ambition. Satan desires power and knowledge and he leads a rebellion against God. For this, he is thrown out of heaven into hell.

How does Shelley relate Frankenstein to *Paradise Lost*?

The Preface links *Frankenstein* to *Paradise Lost*, and Shelley uses many references to it in the novel.

Like *Paradise Lost*, *Frankenstein* is a creation story. Victor resembles Satan in his thirst for forbidden knowledge and his ambition to know and control the source of life. He hoped that 'A new species would bless me as its creator'. However, his creation is monstrous and he is punished when his family and friends are destroyed.

The Creature reads *Paradise Lost* when he is living in the forest; in it, he finds links between the story and his own situation. At first, he compares himself to Adam, brought to life by one creator. He says to Victor 'I ought to be thy Adam'. Later, he thinks Satan a 'fitter emblem' for his own situation, for 'like him, when I viewed the bliss of my protectors, a bitter gall of envy rose within me'. He concluded that his situation was worse than Satan's, because Satan had friends whereas the Creature is 'solitary and abhorred'.

The Creature argues that Victor should take responsibility for him, as Victor is his maker. Victor is almost persuaded of this, until he remembers the Creature has murdered and has committed himself to evil, like Satan.

At the end, when the Creature weeps over Victor's corpse, he again refers to Satan: 'the fallen angel becomes a malignant devil'. The Creature feels that he was doomed to be miserable by the circumstances of his birth. For this he blames his creator: Victor intended to create an Adam but instead created a Satan.

Key Quotations to Learn

'I ought to be thy Adam, but I am rather the fallen angel,' (The Creature: Chapter 10)

'Satan has his companions, fellow-devils, to admire and encourage him; but I am solitary and abhorred.' (The Creature: Chapter 15)

I was cursed by some devil, and carried about with me my eternal hell; (Victor: Chapter 24)

Summary

- Shelley uses many references to *Paradise Lost* in the novel.
- Like God creating Adam, Victor creates a being.
- Like Satan, Victor's ambition and desire for knowledge leads to his downfall.
- The Creature, like Satan, envies humans for their happiness and ability to love.

Sample Analysis

The Creature is a powerful orator and references *Paradise Lost* and the Bible to add weight to his arguments. He says 'I remembered Adam's supplication to his Creator. But where was mine?' The word 'supplication', meaning prayer, shows his erudition. He tends to use more learned, older words, rather than modern ones, for example, he addresses Victor as 'creator' and uses 'thy' and 'thou', archaic forms that add solemnity to his argument.

Questions

QUICK TEST
1. Where is the first mention of *Paradise Lost* in the novel?
2. In what way does Victor resemble Satan?
3. Why does the Creature at first think he resembles Adam?

EXAM PRACTICE
Using one or more of the 'Key Quotations to Learn', write a paragraph analysing how Shelley uses themes from *Paradise Lost* in the novel.

Victor Frankenstein

You must be able to: analyse how Victor Frankenstein is presented in the novel.

Is Victor a hero or a victim?

When Walton meets him, Victor is broken, physically and emotionally, yet Walton's impression of Victor is that he is a noble, heroic soul brought low. Victor's story is the main part of the novel and we learn of events and about the characters through Victor.

As Victor tells it, his brilliant career as a scientist was ended by destiny and he has suffered terrible loss as a result. Victor wants us to think of him as a victim of events beyond his own control. But we should ask how far Victor caused his own problems and how far he is willing to admit this. He has moments of self-knowledge but these insights do not last.

What are his fatal flaws?

Victor tells us he had obsessive tendencies as a child. His burning ambition to pursue scientific knowledge also shows this. He dreams of glory but this backfires when he sees the Creature, a hideous embodiment of his failed ambitions.

Though physically unimposing, Victor has great personal charm that impresses Walton. His close relationships with Clerval and Elizabeth show that he is affectionate and has a strong emotional side. He is highly sensitive and suffers from long stress-induced illnesses at significant points, for example, after he has brought the Creature to life. He finds ways to distract himself rather than face the consequences of his actions.

Victor is often unable to take action. When he does, it has disastrous consequences. For example, he does not seek revenge on the Creature until the Creature has murdered three times. We might view him as a coward, paralysed by fear and denial. He simply can't face up to what he has done.

Victor is an egotist, seeing himself as someone born to a great mission, but he is unable to see beyond his own point of view. He refuses to acknowledge the Creature at first, horrified at the hideousness of his own creation. This has fatal consequences.

Does Victor change?

Victor's narration to Walton is really a long **confession**, an attempt to set the record straight. However, it does not seem to bring him any ease and, at the end, he remains determined to hunt down and kill the Creature. Some readers sense that Victor repents his misdeeds; others feel that is he is filled only with self-pity.

Key Quotations to Learn

... the beauty of the dream vanished, and breathless horror and disgust filled my heart. (Victor: Chapter 5)

'... my fate is nearly fulfilled.' (Victor: Letter IV)

... so noble a creature, destroyed by misery ... (Walton: Letter IV)

Summary

- Victor presents himself as a **tragic hero** and sometimes as a victim.
- Sometimes he shows self-knowledge; at other times, self-delusion.
- He's affectionate, intelligent and has charm and charisma.
- His **fatal flaws** undermine his natural talents and he's ineffective at facing up to challenges.

Sample Analysis

Victor's treatment of Elizabeth shows his egocentricity. When he goes to university, he cuts her off so completely that she asks him whether he has found someone else. Before they marry, he writes a letter to her saying he has a 'dreadful secret' that he will reveal *after* the wedding. This makes her anxious and depressed in the weeks leading up to the wedding. Finally, even knowing that the Creature has threatened to visit them on their wedding night, he marries her, perhaps hoping the Creature would come for him, but effectively sacrificing Elizabeth to the Creature.

Questions

QUICK TEST
1. Why does Shelley have Victor tell most of the story?
2. What is Walton's view of Victor?
3. What does Victor do rather than face his problems?
4. Why did Victor reject the Creature?

EXAM PRACTICE
Using one or more of the 'Key Quotations to Learn', write a paragraph analysing how Shelley presents Victor as both hero and victim of his own story.

The Creature

You must be able to: analyse how the Creature is presented in the novel.

What does he look like?

The Creature is created from the body parts of dead people, which are collected by Victor. Victor intended to create a beautiful example of humanity – but the Creature is so hideous that he terrifies everyone who sees him. Seeing his own reflection in a pond, the Creature is horrified. He is bigger than a human, moves quickly and is powerful. He's also very good at staying hidden and manages to track Victor's every move, like a hunter.

How is the Creature presented?

As a highly sensitive being born with the capacity to be good, the Creature is presented sympathetically. He is intelligent, well read, self-educated and eloquent. He's presented as a being who appreciates beauty and kindness and wants to improve himself. He helps the cottagers by gathering firewood, and even saves a girl's life, but each time he reaches out to people he is attacked.

He can never be accepted by humans, yet he craves affection and human interaction. This makes him a tragic figure, but he makes a choice to reject 'good' and turn to 'evil'. In revenge for the cottagers' treatment of him, he sets fire to their cottage and dances around it like a **banshee**. Then he vows 'eternal hatred and vengeance to all mankind', and specifically to the person whom he holds responsible for his misery – Victor. He murders William, Henry and Elizabeth and frames Justine.

What is his relationship with Victor?

Although he taunts Victor and makes his life a misery, the Creature is drawn to his creator. Victor is the only human that he *can* approach and speak to. He wants Victor to accept him, but realising this can never be, he makes a vow, 'I will glut the maw of death, until it be satiated with the blood of your remaining friends'. He makes a deal with Victor to disappear if Victor will create a mate for him. When Victor fails to do this, the Creature issues a threat; 'I shall be with you on your wedding night'. Like a ghostly twin or **doppelganger**, the Creature follows Victor's every move. Victor hates and fears the Creature, calling him 'devil' and 'vile insect'. Yet, the Creature regards Victor as his creator until the end and weeps over his corpse. His final speech expresses sorrow, remorse and love. It is a doomed relationship, each unable to forgive the other for what he has done.

Key Quotations to Learn

His limbs were in proportion, and I had selected his features as beautiful. Beautiful! (Victor: Chapter 5)

'Why did you form a monster so hideous that even *you* turned from me in disgust?' (The Creature: Chapter 15)

'I was benevolent and good; misery made me a fiend. Make me happy, and I shall again be virtuous.' (The Creature: Chapter 10)

Summary

- The Creature feels cursed by his hideous appearance.
- He blames Victor for this.
- His attempts to better himself and to do good cause him only more misery.
- His response to hatred and misery is revenge.

Sample Analysis

The Creature is an impressive speaker. When he says, 'You, my creator, abhor me; what hope can I gather from your fellow-creatures, who owe me nothing? They spurn and hate me', he uses learned, **Latinate** and Biblical vocabulary: 'creator' is a reference to the creation story in the Old Testament. It reminds Victor that he has 'played God'. He likes to use **rhetorical questions** as a persuasive device; the **monosyllables** in the second sentence indicate his passionate anger.

Questions

QUICK TEST
1. In what ways is the Creature 'superhuman'?
2. What happens when he reaches out to humans?
3. Why does he set fire to the cottage?
4. How does the Creature react to Victor's death?

EXAM PRACTICE
Using one or more of the 'Key Quotations to Learn', write a paragraph analysing how Shelley presents the Creature's attitude to Victor.

You must be able to: analyse how Robert Walton is presented in the novel.

What is Walton's purpose in the novel?

Walton has an important job to do as chief narrator of the story. All the stories that we read – Victor's, the Creature's, even Safie's story, are told through him. His letters to his sister 'bookend' the novel and give another perspective to Victor's strange and compelling narrative.

It is important that Walton is established at the start of the novel as an ordinary, if romantically minded, man. He is presented as an educated man, vaguely bored with life, in search of adventure.

It's vital that readers believe Walton is telling the truth, as the tale he hears from Victor is quite incredible. However, telling the truth does not mean he is unbiased.

Are Walton and Victor similar?

Walton's 'great enterprise' is to travel to the North Pole. He hopes to achieve glory in this, and later we learn that Victor's ambition was similarly fuelled by dreams of fame and glory.

Important parallels are drawn between Walton's situation – he's stuck in the ice and thwarted from his purpose – and Victor, who was also ambitious for glory in his youth but is now also stuck in the icy wastes in a relentless pursuit of the Creature. At the end, Walton accepts his own failure and turns for home. This is something Victor cannot do. Walton is therefore presented as more rational and sensible than Victor, although less firm of purpose.

How does Walton relate to Victor?

Walton instantly likes Victor – this is because Walton has few close friends and feels no closeness with the ship's crew. There's a certain snobbishness in his attraction to Victor, whom he considers 'noble' and educated, and he is willing to accept Victor's vision of himself as some sort of a tragic hero brought low by destiny. This appeals to Walton's Romantic nature.

How does Walton relate to the Creature?

It is important that Shelley chose to have Walton meet the Creature face to face at the end of the novel. First, it tells readers that Victor is not mad: the Creature really did exist. Second, we read the Creature's own words as spoken to Walton, not through Victor this time. When he meets the Creature, Walton wavers between accusing him of hypocrisy and feeling sympathy for his plight. In this respect, he is in a similar position to readers of the novel.

Key Quotations to Learn

And now, my dear Margaret, do I not deserve to accomplish some great purpose? (Walton: Letter I)

Margaret, what comment can I make on the untimely extinction of this glorious spirit? (Walton, in Continuation, September 12th)

Thus are my hopes blasted by cowardice and indecision; (Walton, in Continuation, September 7th)

Summary

- Walton's letters to his sister frame Victor's narrative.
- These provide a rational backdrop to Victor's strange and fantastic tale.
- Walton's situation establishes important themes that are later explored, such as pursuit of personal glory, the value of scientific exploration and the need for friendship.
- He is the last person to speak to the Creature.

Sample Analysis

Walton has similarities with Victor and the Creature. Like the Creature, he's lonely, 'I desire the company of a man who could sympathise with me' and he's self-educated, 'for the first fourteen years of my life I ran wild on a common'. Like Victor, he has ambitions to achieve a 'great enterprise'. To modern readers, Walton's effusive tone when he speaks of Victor's nobility might sound insincere but his mode of expression is typical of Romantic poetry; interestingly, he likens himself to the 'Ancient Mariner' of Coleridge's poem *The Rime of the Ancient Mariner* at the end of Letter II.

Questions

QUICK TEST
1. What does Walton admire about Victor?
2. Why has Walton decided to go to the North Pole?
3. When does Walton speak to the Creature?
4. Why does Walton turn for home?

EXAM PRACTICE
Using one or more of the 'Key Quotations to Learn', write a paragraph analysing the similarities between Walton and Victor.

Henry Clerval

You must be able to: analyse how Henry Clerval is presented in the novel.

What is Henry's purpose in the novel?

Henry Clerval is Victor's closest friend. He is presented as a **foil** to Victor in character, temperament and tastes. Henry's interests are romantic and imaginative; he has no interest in science. He is calm, reasonable and even-tempered. He is not prone to obsession or depression like Victor. At several points in the novel when Victor is in trouble, ill or depressed, Henry is there to offer help, comfort and sympathy. For example, he is the first person Victor talks to after giving life to the Creature, calming Victor down. In a sense, for Victor, Henry comes to represent everything that was good about his own life before the Creature was created.

How does Shelley use Henry to represent virtue?

Henry is not presented as a complex, rounded character. He is there to represent sanity, normality, good humour and virtue, in comparison with Victor's unbalanced reactions. Henry is also refined, well-mannered and handsome. Therefore, Henry is presented as the exact opposite of the Creature. Henry is an example of how good birth, a happy childhood, good education and healthy socialisation can create virtue and the desire to do good – and all these things are the polar opposite of the Creature's experiences.

What is significant about Henry's death?

The Creature murders three people in the novel, all innocent of any crime. First, William, Victor's younger brother, then Henry, his closest friend, and finally, Elizabeth, his wife. Each of the murders is intended to hurt Victor by taking away his emotional support. The Creature strangles Henry in revenge after Victor destroys the She-Creature. Henry's death throws Victor into a convulsive fit that almost kills him.

Key Quotations to Learn

Alas, how great was the contrast between us! (Victor: Chapter 18)

Clerval! Beloved friend! ... He was a being formed in the 'very poetry of nature.' (Victor: Chapter 18)

His soul overflowed with ardent affections, (Victor: Chapter 18)

Summary

- Clerval represents moral virtue, love and sympathy, humanity and benevolence in the novel.
- His interests and personality contrast with Victor's.
- His fortunate background and virtuous character contrast with the Creature's.

Sample Analysis

Henry is a loyal friend to Victor; he is the first person Victor sees after giving life to the Creature and his affable nature offers solace when Victor is depressed, 'Henry soothed me'. Although he suspects something is wrong, Henry respects Victor's privacy: 'he never attempted to draw my secret' and the Creature creates a distance between the two friends because Victor can never tell Henry what he has done. This makes Victor's anguish at Clerval's death all the more painful, 'Clerval, my friend and dearest companion, had fallen victim to me'.

Questions

QUICK TEST
1. Give one example of when Henry comes to Victor's aid at a stressful time.
2. What does Henry represent?
3. How do Henry's interests differ from Victor's?
4. How does the Creature kill Henry?

EXAM PRACTICE
Using one or more of the 'Key Quotations to Learn', write a paragraph analysing why Shelley used Henry's character to show the beneficial effects of a loving family and good upbringing.

Elizabeth Lavenza, Caroline and Alphonse Frankenstein, Justine Moritz

You must be able to: analyse how these characters are presented in the novel.

What qualities does Shelley present though Elizabeth?

Elizabeth is adopted by the Frankensteins but is of noble birth. She's idealised by Victor as 'celestial', a 'cherub' and for him she represents his happy life before it became tainted by the Creature. Shelley does not develop Elizabeth into a complex character: she is a **symbol** of goodness and virtue. As such, she is rather one-dimensional and passive. Her one act of decisiveness is when she speaks out in defence of Justine at her trial. She is the Creature's final victim, on her wedding night.

What do Caroline and Alphonse Frankenstein represent?

Victor's parents are also idealised by Victor. Victor's mother dies of scarlet fever when he is 17 years old and his grief following this event prompts him to leave for university. Her death represents the end of Victor's childhood.

His father is a dependable source of love and affection for Victor. He dies of grief following the murder of Elizabeth and this is the catalyst for Victor to pursue the Creature and kill him. Alphonse represents benevolent fatherly love, in contrast to the lack of affection that Victor feels for the Creature – for example, Alphonse travels to Ireland to speak on his son's behalf at the trial.

What is the significance of Justine Moritz?

Justine has a small but important part to play in the story. She is framed by the Creature and stands trial for William's murder. Although innocent, she confesses to the crime and is hanged – in contrast to Victor, who cannot admit to his wrongdoing. The injustice of Justine's death, and his sense that he is to blame because the Creature is the real murderer, sends Victor into a deep depression.

Key Quotations to Learn

I was their plaything and their idol, and something better – their child, (Victor: Chapter 1)

... a being heaven-sent, and bearing a celestial stamp in all her features. (Victor, referring to Justine: Chapter 1)

... William and Justine, the first hapless victims to my unhallowed arts. (Victor: Chapter 8)

Summary

- Shelley presents these minor characters as symbolic rather than rounded or complex.
- They represent goodness, virtue, love and benevolence.
- What happens to Justine (her name is a clue) is an example of the injustice of the criminal justice system.

Sample Analysis

Justine's final words, 'Live, and be happy, and make others so' offer a stark contrast to the curses and threats uttered by Victor and the Creature. They represent the happy life and outlook that Victor had before he formed the Creature, and the life that the Creature longs to have, but cannot.

Questions

QUICK TEST
1. What is Victor's view of Elizabeth?
2. Give an example of paternal love shown by Alphonse Frankenstein.
3. Where does Victor go after his mother dies?
4. What is Justine's punishment?

EXAM PRACTICE
Using one or more of the 'Key Quotations to Learn', write a paragraph analysing why Shelley chose to present Victor's parents and Elizabeth as idealised, one-dimensional characters.

You must be able to: analyse how these characters are presented in the novel.

What do the De Laceys represent to the Creature?

The Creature regards the De Lacey family as ideal representatives of the human race. He regards them as wondrous beings. By observing them, he learns about human society, values, communication and the power of family affection. Given his earlier unhappy encounters with society, it is to his credit that the Creature can appreciate the finer feelings and emotions of the De Lacey family.

The cottagers are idealised by the Creature and we learn of them only through him. Therefore, they are not drawn as complex characters. They, like the Creature, are outsiders, exiled from their native France. He calls them his 'protectors' and regards them almost as an adopted family.

The De Lacey family deepens the Creature's longing to be part of human society. Their rejection of him dispels any hope of this forever. It is a bitter blow for him and he never again attempts to integrate with humans. Shortly afterwards, the Creature decides to follow a path of evil and destruction.

What is the significance of Safie's history?

Shelley chose to include Safie's history right at the centre of the book. Therefore, Safie's story must have significance. It contains themes that are echoed elsewhere in the novel. Like the Creature, Safie, being Arabian, is an outsider in this society. Her mother was also an outsider who married out of her culture. Safie's story is about how love can overcome barriers of race, distance and society. This increases the Creature's desire to love and be loved in return, and prompts him to ask Victor to create a female Creature for him to love.

As an outsider, Safie has to learn a new language. The Creature, hidden, educates himself alongside her. This means that when he finds some books and Victor's lab notes, he learns about how man, and he himself, were created – things that he afterwards wishes he had never known.

Key Quotations to Learn

I looked upon them as superior beings, who would be the arbiters of my future destiny. (The Creature: Chapter 12)

… a countenance of angelic beauty and expression. (The Creature describing Felix seeing Safie: Chapter 13)

My protectors had departed, and had broken the only link that held me to the world. (The Creature: Chapter 16)

Summary

- To the Creature, the cottagers represent an ideal human society.
- Though poor, they are presented as symbols of happiness, goodness and wisdom.
- They intensify the Creature's craving to be part of society and his misery that he never will be.
- Safie's story has echoes of several of the novel's themes.

Sample Analysis

The Creature uses different terms to refer to the cottagers. At first, they are 'lovely creatures' and 'superior beings' that he observes almost in the manner of a science experiment, wanting to understand their relationships and behaviour. Later, they become 'my friends', 'my protectors' and 'my beloved cottagers', showing how he grows to identify with them (the **possessive adjective** 'my' indicates this) and feels close to them, even though the relationship is all in his own mind; his feelings for them are not reciprocated at all.

Questions

QUICK TEST
1. What does the Creature learn from observing the family?
2. Why is the family living in the forest?
3. Why does the Creature idealise the family?
4. How does the arrival of Safie change the Creature's life?

EXAM PRACTICE
Using one or more of the 'Key Quotations to Learn', write a paragraph analysing the part that the De Lacey family play in the novel.

Justice and Revenge

You must be able to: analyse how Shelley explores justice and revenge in the novel.

How does Shelley present justice in the novel?

Shelley presents two kinds of justice in the novel: human or man-made criminal justice in the form of court trials and natural justice in the form of the Creature seeking retribution on Victor.

In several places, legal justice is shown to be flawed. Justine Moritz is tried for the murder of William. She confesses, is found guilty, and is hanged. Safie's father was sentenced unjustly. When Victor confesses to a magistrate, he is not believed.

Shelley invites readers to speculate about the limits of legal justice. Should man have the power to decide whether a human should live or die? Man sometimes gets justice wrong.

How is revenge shown in the novel?

At several points, the Creature talks of the 'injustice' of his situation: he, who wanted to be virtuous, was spurned, 'kicked and trampled on' by humans. He says, 'Even now my blood boils at the recollection of this injustice'. He desires revenge on Victor for this. He holds Victor responsible, and to his mind Victor failed in his responsibilities when he abandoned and disowned him. The Creature's first act of pure revenge is when he burns down the De Laceys' cottage in retribution for their rejection of him.

Did Shelley intend us to sympathise with the Creature's point of view? Do his actions offer a moral lesson on what happens if we have no recourse to legal justice? In his situation, is revenge justified, or is it always wrong?

Victor's attitude is influenced by what happened to Justine and he swears revenge on the Creature, yet he retains a belief in legal justice until the magistrate refuses to believe his story. Then, he too decides he has no option but to take justice into his own hands and kill the Creature himself.

Key Quotations to Learn

'I will revenge my injuries: if I cannot inspire love, I will cause fear,'
(The Creature: Chapter 17)

'Am I to be thought the only criminal, when all human kind has **sinned** against me?'
(The Creature: Walton, in Continuation, September 12th)

... I swear to pursue the demon who caused this misery, until he or I shall perish in mortal conflict. (Victor: Chapter 24)

Summary

- Shelley presents criminal justice in the trial of Justine (her name is a clue).
- Justine is found guilty through what Victor calls a 'wretched mockery of justice'.
- The Creature wants revenge because he feels man, especially Victor, has treated him unjustly.

Sample Analysis

In the Creature, Shelley presents a being who feels injustice very strongly. His first life experience was rejection from a parental figure and this set him up for a lifetime of rejection. When the Creature says, 'You accuse me of murder; and yet you would, with a satisfied conscience, destroy your own creature. Oh, praise the eternal justice of man!' he is being **sarcastic**. He accuses Victor of hypocrisy for wishing to destroy the murderer that he himself is responsible for creating. The words 'satisfied conscience' are ironic, for where was Victor's conscience when he decided to give him life? Justice demanded that Justine be hanged in retribution for William's murder. The Creature is reminding Victor of this. To the Creature, as all of humankind has sinned against him, revenge is justified.

Questions

QUICK TEST

1. Which characters are put on trial in the novel?
2. What phrase does Victor use to describe the outcome of Justine's trial?
3. What do both the Creature and Victor decide to do as a result of their experience with human justice?

EXAM PRACTICE

Using one or more of the 'Key Quotations to Learn', write a paragraph analysing how Shelley presents justice in the novel.

Nature

You must be able to: analyse how Shelley presents the theme of nature in the novel.

Why was nature important to Shelley?

Shelley's view of nature was influenced by the Romantic Movement. Romantic writers presented natural beauty as awe-inspiring, with a power that enabled people to momentarily transcend their own existence. They used the word 'sublime' to express this. The majesty and glory of nature could uplift the soul and fire the imagination, but nature was not always benign or even friendly. Hostile environments such as icy, bleak and mountainous landscapes were revered for their raw and terrifying power. Shelley often personifies nature as female – another trait of Romantic writers.

Which characters respond to nature in a Romantic way?

Victor, Walton and the Creature are emotionally moved by natural beauty in ways that would have been familiar to the Romantic imagination. Victor's spirits are lifted when he witnesses an Alpine storm, before the Creature arrives and spoils the mood. The Creature's sensitivity to natural beauty is shown when he recalls how the arrival of spring in the forest made him feel happy.

The Creature presents a contradiction. Though he responds to nature as a Romantic, the manner of his creation was unnatural – in fact, he is man-made. His abnormally hideous exterior inspires terror rather than awe, yet his soul is capable of good. While he can survive in the natural world, he is a supernatural being beyond human or scientific understanding.

Victor admires nature but seeks to control it by science and this unnatural activity unleashes a supernatural power that he cannot control. It kills his family, his friends and himself. It is ironic that an icy landscape, the same kind he admired as a child, is where he dies after the Creature has led him, tauntingly, through some of the most hostile environments on Earth.

How does nature feature in the novel?

Important moments in the novel often take place in bleak and isolated spots that are terrifying but magnificent. Victor meets the Creature in the Alps. Walton meets Victor on the ice near the North Pole. Victor goes to Orkney to create the She-Creature.

In the novel, cold and dark symbolise isolation, danger and even death; warmth and light represent life, happiness and friendship. When Victor gives life to the creature, it is a '... dreary night of November ...'. Compare this with the sunlit, green countryside of Victor's childhood.

Key Quotations to Learn

... I pursued nature to her hiding places. (Victor: Chapter 4)

These sublime and magnificent scenes afforded me the greatest consolation ... (Victor: Chapter 10)

'Happy, happy earth! fit habitation for gods,' (The Creature: Chapter 12)

Summary

- Typically for a Romantic writer, Shelley personifies nature as female.
- Characters respond emotionally to nature's power.
- Shelley chooses to set important scenes in cold, isolated and hostile environments.
- The Creature's birth was unnatural; Victor sought to control nature by science.
- The Creature punishes Victor by leading him through hostile terrain.

Sample Analysis

Shelley uses natural language to create a link between Victor and nature: for example, in Chapter 2, Victor likens the birth of his passion for science to a 'mountain river' that 'swept away all my hopes and joys'. For Victor, and for the Romantics, nature's divine grandeur had restorative powers: he describes the Alpine air as 'salubrious' – the literal meaning is 'health-giving'. Nature consoles Victor in a way that his family and friends do not.

Questions

QUICK TEST
1. Which group of people influenced Shelley's presentation of nature?
2. What technique does Shelley use to write about nature?
3. Which word did writers use to express the uplifting power of nature?
4. How does the Creature respond to nature?

EXAM PRACTICE
Using one of the 'Key Quotations to Learn', write a paragraph analysing how Shelley presents nature's power in the novel.

Scientific Knowledge

You must be able to: analyse how Shelley presents scientific knowledge in the novel.

Was Shelley influenced by scientific theories?

Shelley was acquainted with popular scientific theories of the time. 'Galvanism' was one of these. It was also known as 'animal electricity' because laboratory experiments had shown that an electric current passed through a muscle would cause it to contract.

How is galvanism shown in *Frankenstein*?

Victor's interest in galvanism begins when he witnesses a thunderstorm when he is 15 years old. He sees the power of nature when electricity destroys a tree during a thunderstorm. Although the details of the Creature's birth are not described in detail, Shelley hints that Victor uses galvanism to create him.

How does Shelley present science in the novel?

Two men – Walton the explorer and Frankenstein the chemist – show the negative side of man's thirst for scientific knowledge. Both are motivated by personal glory and power that they think will be theirs as a result of scientific discovery. Victor says, '... I will pioneer a new way, explore unknown powers, and unfold to the world the mysteries of creation.' In contrast, Henry Clerval is a **Humanist** with no interest in science.

Perhaps Shelley is suggesting that man is arrogant to think he can control nature through science. This would fit with the Romantic view that nature and the natural world contain mysteries that man should not try to understand: nature's power should command man's respect.

Does *Frankenstein* present a warning against scientific enquiry?

It does not follow that Shelley's story is anti-science. Science itself has no conscience or moral compass. Perhaps Shelley is saying that man has a responsibility to use scientific discovery for the good of mankind. Victor is brilliant and his hideous creation is in many ways truly amazing, but his motivation was wrong and he pays a high price for his ambition.

In presenting the Creature as a sensitive, intelligent and eloquent being who had the power to be good before he turned to evil, Shelley shows that even misguided scientific experiments have the potential to do good, if they are handled responsibly.

Key Quotations to Learn

How dangerous is the acquirement of knowledge and how much happier that man is who believes his native town to be the world, than he who aspires to be greater than his nature will allow. (Victor: Chapter 4)

One man's life or death were but a small price to pay for the acquirement of knowledge which I sought; (Walton: Letter IV)

Summary

- Shelley was influenced by scientific theories of the time, including galvanism.
- It is possible that Victor used galvanism to give life to the Creature.
- Shelley's presentation of man's pursuit of scientific discovery is complex.
- The Creature can be viewed as a scientific experiment gone wrong.
- Victor is a brilliant scientist but lacks maturity and responsibility.

Questions

QUICK TEST
1. Which two characters pursue scientific enquiry?
2. Which scientific theory does Victor probably use to bring the Creature to life?
3. Which event sparked young Victor's interest in the power of electricity?

EXAM PRACTICE
Using one of the 'Key Quotations to Learn', write a paragraph analysing how Shelley presents scientific knowledge in the novel.

Family and Society

You must be able to: analyse how Shelley explores family and society in the novel.

How is family presented in *Frankenstein*?

Family relationships are presented positively in *Frankenstein*. Having a close and loving family is shown to be a source of emotional comfort for several characters.

The novel starts with Walton's letters to his sister Margaret, who is concerned for his welfare.

Victor tells Walton that his childhood was idyllic. He was doted on by his parents: 'they seemed to draw inexhaustible stores of affection from the very mine of love to bestow them on me'. The Frankensteins adopted Elizabeth when Victor was five and she was adored by the whole family. Victor was very close to his mother and was devastated when she died of scarlet fever.

When the Creature observes the closeness and affection the cottagers have for each other, he is struck by 'sensations of [...] a peculiar and overpowering nature: they were a mixture of pain and pleasure,'. He grows to love their kindness and gentleness. He calls them his 'protectors'. He is drawn to make himself known to them because he craves the affection he has observed in their family relationships.

The Creature has no family. He reproaches Victor for abandoning him, '... I learned from your papers that you were my father, my creator.'

How is society presented?

Society is presented both positively and negatively in *Frankenstein*. The Creature is not accepted by human society because of his monstrous appearance: 'Was I then a monster, a blot upon the earth, from which all men fled, and whom all men disowned?' but he desperately wants to be part of human society.

Both Victor and the Creature are outsiders from society: Victor isolates himself to perform his experiments, and because of his hideous appearance the Creature is forced to remain hidden from general society.

Alienation from society makes the Creature miserable – he says '... what a wretched outcast I was.' When Victor is with his family or his friend Clerval, his life is happier. When isolated, Victor falls into depression and, often, illness.

Walton too is lonely. He writes that he has no close friend on the ship and he feels distant from the crew. This partly explains why he instantly forms a close bond with Frankenstein. He says, 'I begin to love him [Victor] as a brother'.

Key Quotations to Learn

'What chiefly struck me was the gentle manners of these people; and I longed to join them, but dared not.' (The Creature: Chapter 12)

'But where were my friends and relations? No father had watched my infant days, no mother had blessed me with smiles ...' (The Creature: Chapter 13)

'My protectors had departed, and had broken the only link that held me to the world.' (The Creature: Chapter 16)

Summary

- The Frankenstein family and the cottagers are examples of the benefits of a happy family life.
- The Creature yearns to be part of a family and to be accepted by society.
- Victor and the Creature show the negative effects of isolation.

Sample Analysis

The Creature's view of family love can be seen by his reaction to rejection by the cottagers. He says 'I could have torn him (Felix) limb from limb as the lion rends the antelope. But my heart sunk within me as with bitter sickness, and I refrained'. This suggests the conflict he feels between violent anger in self-defence and misery that the people he wants so much to accept him, will not. His words are violent and shocking and his use of a natural **simile** of wild animals suggests his own natural power.

Questions

QUICK TEST
1. How is the Frankenstein family presented?
2. What word does the Creature use to show his relationship with the De Laceys?
3. At what points in the story does Victor isolate himself?

EXAM PRACTICE
Using one or more of the 'Key Quotations to Learn', write a paragraph analysing how Shelley presents the desire for affection and acceptance in the novel.

Gothic Themes

You must be able to: analyse how Shelley uses Gothic themes in the novel.

What are some Gothic themes that Shelley includes in *Frankenstein*?

Gothic novels explored the 'dark' side of life: mystery, death, danger and the supernatural, and intended to horrify, shock and terrify readers. Shelley uses several Gothic themes in her novel including revenge, good versus evil, villain and victim, violence and bloodthirsty acts. The Creature is composed of corpses – death – and he is created in mysterious circumstances, at night, in the darkness. The Creature's thirst for bloodthirsty revenge is a constant source of danger for Victor. His threat 'I shall be with you on your wedding night' hangs like a curse over Victor's wedding to Elizabeth.

What is Gothic about the Creature?

Chapter 5 starts 'It was on a gloomy night in November' and the word 'gloomy', which means dull, sets a mood of mystery and prepares the reader for the horrifying events that follow when Victor raises the Creature from the dead. By the light of a 'half-extinguished' candle, Victor remembers, '... I saw the dull yellow eye of the creature open ...' and says the skin too was yellow, the eyes 'watery' the complexion 'shrivelled' and with 'straight black lips'. This is a horrifying description.

What is Gothic about Victor?

It could be said that Victor behaves more like a female Gothic character than a male one. In Gothic fiction, the heroines are often victims who have a tendency to faint and need to be rescued – Victor faints at the sight of Clerval's dead body (it 'passed like a dream from my memory'). Gothic heroines have an overactive imagination: when Victor goes back to the laboratory, he thinks he sees 'the dreaded spectre glide into the room' and 'imagined that the monster seized me'. He falls into a fit and does not recover for a long time.

What about the women in the novel?

Women are presented in a way that is typical of Gothic fiction: they are passive victims, placed in dangerous situations. Caroline Frankenstein dies of a fatal illness, Justine is framed for a murder and executed, Elizabeth is powerless and violently murdered, and Safie is victimised.

Key Quotations to Learn

Who shall conceive the horrors of my secret toil as I dabbled among the unhallowed damps of the grave or tortured the living animal to animate the lifeless clay? My limbs now tremble and my eyes swim with the remembrance; (Victor: Chapter 4)

Oh! No mortal could support the horror of that countenance. (Victor: Chapter 5)

My heart palpitated in the sickness of fear; (Victor: Chapter 5)

Summary

- Shelley uses key elements of Gothic fiction to inspire horror and terror in readers.
- The Creature is horrifying to look at, was born in the dark and is made of body parts of dead people.
- The Creature commits violent, bloodthirsty murders.

Sample Analysis

Shelley's presentation of Gothic horror and terror is shown when Victor first reacts to the Creature. He calls the event a 'catastrophe' and the colour **adjectives** he uses to describe the appearance of the Creature tell us of his horror – 'watery eye', 'yellow skin', 'dun white sockets', 'black hair' and 'thin, black lips'. Shelley also uses **exclamations** 'Great God!' and 'Beautiful!' to show the strength of Victor's reaction. He falls asleep and dreams of embracing his dead mother but there are worms in her shroud, showing that his mind is disturbed.

Questions

QUICK TEST
1. What is the atmosphere on the night of the Creature's birth?
2. How does Victor react when he sees Clerval's dead body?
3. At what point does Victor think he sees the Creature's ghost?
4. What is 'Gothic' about the way Shelley presents women in the novel?

EXAM PRACTICE
Using one or more of the 'Key Quotations to Learn', write a paragraph analysing how Shelley uses Gothic themes in the novel.

You must be able to: analyse how Shelley explores the idea of heroism in the novel.

What is a hero?

In literature, a **hero** is someone whose actions and qualities are admired. A hero possesses courage, resilience and outstanding personal virtues. A tragic hero is someone with a noble character but whose fatal flaw results in his/her downfall.

Are there heroes in *Frankenstein*?

Victor presents Clerval as a noble being of heroic worth – someone to be looked up to and admired. But he presents himself to Walton as a tragic hero, someone whom destiny has brought low. Walton sees his voyage to the North Pole as a glorious, heroic expedition. Both men talk of their hopes, in a way that is exaggeratedly emotional, **grandiose** and heroic.

Walton and Victor are examples of flawed heroes. They do not act in a classically heroic way, despite what they say: Walton abandons his voyage; Victor fails to take responsibility for the consequences of his own actions, and for much of the novel, he evades problems, rather than facing them.

The Creature can be seen as a tragic hero – someone who is essentially good but who turns to evil because his 'fatal flaw' (his appearance) alienates him from society: 'I was benevolent ... but am I not alone, miserably alone?' He did not have the advantages of Clerval, Walton or Victor but was destined from birth to be miserable.

How does this link to the subtitle, *A Modern Prometheus*?

In Greek mythology, Prometheus stole fire from the gods to give it to mankind. For this act of rebellion, he was punished by being chained to a rock. Prometheus is now known as the god of fire and, as saviour of mankind, a hero.

Victor's grand vision of becoming immortal by creating life echoes the Prometheus myth. He also steals fire, wishing to 'infuse a spark of being into the lifeless' and he too was punished – ironically, by the Creature he brought to life.

Key Quotations to Learn

'... my fate is nearly fulfilled ... nothing can alter my destiny;' (Victor: Letter IV)

'But such is not my destiny; I must pursue and destroy the being to whom I gave existence;' (Victor: Chapter 24)

'Yet mine shall not be the submission of abject slavery. I will revenge my injuries;' (The Creature: Chapter 17)

Summary

* Walton, Victor and the Creature are examples of the Romantic hero.
* Victor and the Creature can be viewed as tragic heroes.
* Both Victor and the Creature are brought down by fatal flaws.

Sample Analysis

Victor's words to the crew present heroism as showing courage in the face of adversity: 'Do not return to your families with the stigma of disgrace marked on your brows. Return as heroes who have fought and conquered, and who know not what it is to turn their backs on the foe'. His words are fine **rhetoric** intended to raise their spirits. However, it does not work on the crew, which decides to turn back. There is an irony in Victor's fine words, for with his single-minded ambition he created a being with the mark (stigma) of his (Victor's) disgrace. That being returned to haunt him and destroyed his family. These words show that Victor's concept of heroism is flawed and that he has learned nothing from his experiences.

Questions

QUICK TEST
1. In what way can Victor be viewed as a tragic hero?
2. What is the subtitle of the book?
3. How does Victor present the concept of heroism to the sailors?

EXAM PRACTICE
Using one or more of the 'Key Quotations to Learn', write a paragraph analysing how Shelley explores the concept of the hero in the novel.

Nature Versus Nurture

You must be able to: analyse how Shelley explores ideas about nature versus nurture in the novel.

What is 'nature versus nurture'?

Nature refers to our inherited or genetic qualities, including our physical appearance and personality. Nurture means the behaviours that we learn as we grow up. The 'nature versus nurture' debate centres on the question of which has more influence on behaviour: our inherited characteristics or our life experiences.

Does Shelley present both sides of the debate?

Through the Creature, Shelley explores the theme of nature vs nurture. How far is the Creature's behaviour caused by his upbringing and experience of the world, and how far is it inherent in his character?

In Victor, Shelley presents someone who behaves badly and is tortured by guilt. How far is Victor's behaviour due to his nature and how far is it influenced by his upbringing and education?

How does the Creature represent nature versus nurture?

The Creature's birth was unnatural in the sense that it is the result of an experiment, and he had no guiding hand in his life. He was abandoned in an unfamiliar world and finds that he is one of a kind. He had to find his own way and he taught himself to read and speak. Having no point of reference besides a slim collection of books, his experience taught him that he is alien to society, learning about his own birth through Victor's notebooks. He observed a family, and that was his only link with human society.

Even without parents or carers, a formal education, or a family or a society to support and guide him, the Creature might still, through his own efforts, have been a good person, but because he never got the chance to integrate into human society, he was dragged down into evil.

What ideas inform Shelley's presentation of the Creature?

Shelley was influenced by philosophical ideas that were current at the time. According to the Enlightenment philosopher Jean-Jacques Rousseau, humans come 'naturally' into the world with the potential to be good, and would remain good if they were not exposed to the corrupting influence of civilisation. Rousseau coined the term 'noble savage' to describe man in his natural state. Another philosopher, John Locke, put forward the idea of natural man as a 'tabula rasa' or blank slate upon which experience is written to form character. Both ideas underlie Shelley's development of the Creature: 'I was benevolent and good; misery made me a fiend'.

Key Quotations to Learn

'I, the miserable and the abandoned, am an abortion, to be spurned at, and kicked, and trampled on.' (The Creature: Chapter 24)

'I was benevolent and good; misery made me a fiend.' (The Creature: Chapter 10)

Summary

- Shelley represents both sides of the nature versus nurture debate.
- The debate is over the relative importance of innate qualities versus experience in guiding our behaviour.
- In presenting the Creature's development, Shelley draws on philosophical ideas current at the time.

Sample Analysis

Victor says of the Creature, 'He is eloquent and persuasive; ... but trust him not. His soul is as hellish as his form ...'. While he acknowledges that the Creature is educated, Victor does not believe him capable of goodness. This shows that Victor does not believe in the power of nurture to change a person's innate qualities. To Victor, the Creature was born evil and remained evil, in appearance and in character.

Questions

QUICK TEST
1. What is the 'nature versus nurture' debate?
2. In what way does Victor go against his 'nurture'?
3. Why is the Creature dragged down into evil?

EXAM PRACTICE
Using one or more of the 'Key Quotations to Learn', write a paragraph analysing how Shelley explores nature versus nurture in the character of the Creature.

Tips and Assessment Objectives

You must be able to: understand how to approach the exam question and meet the requirements of the mark scheme.

Quick tips

- Read the extract carefully at least twice.

- Make sure you know what the question is asking you. Underline key words and pay attention to the bullet point prompts that come with the questions.

- You will be expected to show that you understand the novel's characters, themes and context.

- Paper 1 is 50 minutes. You should spend about 45 minutes on your *Frankenstein* response. Allow yourself five minutes to plan so there is some structure to your essay.

- All your paragraphs should contain a clear idea, a relevant reference to the novel (ideally a quotation) and analysis of how Shelley conveys this idea. Whenever possible, you should link your comments to the novel's context.

- It can sometimes help, after each paragraph, to quickly re-read the question to keep yourself focussed on the exam task.

- Keep your writing concise. If you waste time 'waffling', you won't be able to include the full range of analysis and understanding that the mark scheme requires.

- It is a good idea to remember what the mark scheme is asking of you.

AO1: Understand and respond to the novel (12 marks)

This is all about coming up with a range of points that match the question, supporting your ideas with references from the novel and writing your essay in a mature, academic style.

Lower	Middle	Upper
The essay has some good ideas that are mostly relevant. Some quotations and references are used to support the ideas.	A clear essay that always focusses on the exam question. Quotations and references support ideas effectively. The response refers to different points in the novel.	A convincing, well-structured essay that answers the question fully. Quotations and references are well-chosen and integrated into sentences. The response covers the whole novel (not everything, but ideas from all of the text rather than just focussing on one or two sections).

AO2: Analyse effects of Shelley's language, form and structure (12 marks)

You need to comment on how specific words, language techniques, sentence structures, diologue or the narrative structure allow Shelley to get her ideas across to the reader. This could simply be something about a character or a larger idea she is exploring through the text. To achieve this, you will need to have learned good quotations to analyse.

Lower	Middle	Upper
Identification of some different methods used by Shelley to convey meaning. Some subject terminology.	Explanation of Shelley's different methods. Clear understanding of the effects of these methods. Accurate use of subject terminology.	Analysis of the full range of Shelley's methods. Thorough exploration of the effects of these methods. Accurate range of subject terminology.

AO3: Understand the relationship between the novel and its context (6 marks)

For this part of the mark scheme, you need to show your understanding of how the characters or Shelley's ideas relate to when she was writing (early 1800s) or when the novel was set (late 1700s).

Lower	Middle	Upper
Some awareness of how ideas in the novel link to its context.	References to relevant aspects of context show clear understanding.	Exploration is linked to specific aspects of the novel's contexts to show detailed understanding.

1. Read the extract from Letter I that begins 'Six years have passed' and ends 'when theirs are failing' and then answer the question that follows.

    In this extract, Walton writes to his sister Margaret. He has not yet started his voyage and talks of his hopes and plans. Starting with this extract, write about how Shelley presents attitudes to ambition in the novel. Write about:

    *   how Shelley presents Walton's attitude to ambition in this extract

    *   how Shelley presents attitudes to ambition in the novel as a whole.

2. Read the extract from Chapter 5 that begins 'For this I had deprived' and ends 'fixed on me' and then answer the question that follows.

    In this extract, Victor has just succeeded in creating life. Starting with this extract, write about how Shelley presents the character of Victor in the novel. Write about:

    *   how Shelley presents the character of Victor in this extract

    *   how Shelley presents the character of Victor in the novel as a whole.

3. Read the extract from Chapter 8 that begins 'Justine assumed an air' and ends 'again be heard!' and then answer the question that follows.

    In this extract, Justine is hanged for a crime she did not commit. Starting with this extract, write about how Shelley presents attitudes to justice in the novel. Write about:

    *   how Shelley presents attitudes to justice in this extract

    *   how Shelley presents attitudes to justice in the novel as a whole.

4. Read the extract from Letter IV that begins, 'I thank you' and ends 'wrecked it – thus!' and then answer the question that follows.

    In this extract, Victor is about to start his narrative to Walton.

    Starting with this extract, write about how Shelley presents interlocking narratives in the novel. Write about:

    *   how Shelley presents narratives in this extract

    *   how Shelley presents the interlocking narratives in the novel as a whole.

5. Read the extract from Chapter 10 that begins 'Believe me, Frankenstein' and ends 'work of your hands' and then answer the question that follows.

    In this extract, the Creature entreats Victor to listen to his story. Starting with this extract, write about how Shelley presents the Creature in the novel. Write about:

    *   how Shelley presents the character of the Creature as sympathetic in this extract

    *   how Shelley presents the character of the Creature in the novel as a whole.

6. Read the extract from Chapter 2 that begins 'When I was about fifteen years old' and ends 'could ever be known' and then answer the question that follows.

    In this extract, Victor recalls a natural event that changed his life. Starting with this extract, write about how Shelley presents attitudes towards nature in the novel. Write about:

    *   how Shelley presents Victor's attitude towards nature in this extract

    *   how Shelley presents attitudes towards nature in the novel as a whole.

7. Read the extract from Chapter 17 that begins 'How inconstant are your feelings!' and ends 'scope for your revenge' and then answer the question that follows.

   In this extract, the Creature explains why Victor should create a companion for him. Starting with this extract, write about how Shelley presents the relationship between Victor and the Creature. Write about:

   • how Shelley presents the relationship between Victor and the Creature in this extract

   • how Shelley presents the relationship between Victor and the Creature in the novel as a whole.

8. Read the extract from Chapter 23 that begins 'She left me' and ends 'I fell senseless on the ground' and then answer the question that follows.

   In this extract, Victor finds his murdered wife Elizabeth's dead body. Starting with this extract, write about how Shelley presents Gothic themes in the novel. Write about:

   • how Shelley presents Gothic themes in this extract

   • how Shelley presents Gothic themes in the novel as a whole.

9. Read the extract from Chapter 4 that begins 'Two years passed' and ends 'at the university' and then answer the question that follows.

   In this extract, Victor recalls his days as a student at Ingolstadt University. Starting with this extract, write about how Shelley presents attitudes to scientific discovery in the novel. Write about:

   • how Shelley presents Victor's attitude to scientific discovery in this extract

   • how Shelley presents attitudes to scientific discovery in the novel as a whole.

10. Read the extract from Chapter 2 that begins 'It was my temper' and ends 'filial love' and then answer the question that follows.

    In this extract, Victor recalls his happy childhood. Starting with this extract, write about how Shelley presents the importance of family and friendship in the novel. Write about:

    • how Shelley presents Victor's attitude to family and friendship in this extract

    • how Shelley presents attitudes to family and friendship in the novel as a whole.

11. Read the extract from Chapter 16 that begins 'When I thought of my friends' and ends 'forked and destroying tongues' and then answer the question that follows.

    In this extract, the Creature has just seen the De Lacey family leaving the cottage for the last time. Starting with this extract, write about how Shelley presents the Creature's desire for revenge in the novel. Write about:

    • how Shelley presents the Creature's desire for revenge in this extract

    • how Shelley presents attitudes to revenge in the novel as a whole.

12. Read the extract from Chapter 15 that begins 'Several changes' and ends 'I cursed him'.

    In this extract, the Creature compares the happiness of the cottagers to his own situation. Starting with this extract, write about how Shelley presents ideas about isolation from society. Write about:

    • how Shelley presents the Creature's attitude to isolation from society in this extract

    • how Shelley presents ideas about isolation from society in the novel as a whole.

Planning a Question Response

You must be able to: understand what an exam question is asking you and prepare your response.

How might an exam question be phrased?

A typical exam question will read like this:

Read the extract from Chapter 16 that begins 'When I thought of my friends' and ends 'forked and destroying tongues' and then answer the question that follows.

In this extract, the Creature has just seen the De Lacey family leaving the cottage for the last time. Starting with this extract, write about how Shelley presents the Creature's desire for revenge in the novel. Write about:

- how Shelley presents the Creature's desire for revenge in this extract
- how Shelley presents attitudes to revenge in the novel as a whole. [30 marks]

How do I work out what to do?

The focus of this question is clear: the theme of revenge.

Use the two bullet points to structure your essay. The first point focusses on the Creature's attitudes presented in the extract. You should refer closely to the extract to answer this part. The second bullet point asks you to write about attitudes shown in the novel. Ideally, you will include quotations you have learned in this part of your essay.

For AO1, you need to show a clear understanding of the Creature's attitude based on what he does, how he speaks and how he affects other characters. You also need to show understanding of other characters' attitudes towards revenge.

For AO2, you need to analyse the different ways Shelley's use of language, form and structure help to show readers these attitudes.

You also need to link your answer to the context of the novel to achieve your AO3 marks.

How can I plan my essay?

You have approximately 45 minutes to write your essay.

This isn't long but you should spend the first 5 minutes writing a quick plan. This will help you to focus your thoughts and write a well-structured essay.

Try to come up with five or six ideas. Each of these ideas can then be written up as a paragraph in the essay.

You can plan in whatever way you find most useful. Some students like to just make a quick list of points and then renumber them into a logical order. Spider diagrams are particularly popular; look at the example on the opposite page.

Extract shows the Creature's passion when the cottagers reject him. His violence – 'a rage of anger'

His poetic voice: clouds 'loitered' (personification)/'like a mighty avalanche' (natural simile)

(Context: Romantic poetry)

Revenge links the Creature and Victor 'the devouring and only passion of my soul' (Victor: Chapter 23)

(Context: Gothic literature)

Attitudes towards revenge

Extract shows how the Creature's attitude changes to desire for revenge

'I will revenge my injuries: if I cannot inspire love, I will cause fear;'

The Creature murders Victor's friend and family

'... if you refuse I will glut the maw of death until it be satiated with the blood of your remaining friends.'

(Context: Reign of Terror)

Shelley asks complex questions about revenge and justice. For example, Justine's trial; the Creature's point of view:

'Am I to be thought the only criminal when all mankind sinned against me?'

(Context: French Revolution)

Summary

- Make sure you read the extract and the question carefully so that you know what the focus is.
- Remember to analyse how ideas are conveyed by Shelley.
- Try to relate your ideas to the novel's social and historical context.

Questions

QUICK TEST

1. What key skills do you need to show in your answer?
2. What are the benefits of writing a quick plan for your essay?
3. Why is it important to read the extract carefully?

EXAM PRACTICE

Plan a response to the following exam question:

Read the extract from Chapter 4 that begins 'Two years passed' and ends 'at the university' and then answer the question that follows.

In this extract, Victor recalls his days as a student at Ingolstadt University. Starting with this extract, write about how Shelley presents attitudes to scientific discovery in the novel. Write about:

- how Shelley presents Victor's attitude to scientific discovery in this extract
- how Shelley presents attitudes to scientific discovery in the novel as a whole.

[30 marks]

Grade 5 Annotated Response

Read the extract from Chapter 16 that begins 'When I thought of my friends' and ends 'forked and destroying tongues' and then answer the question that follows.

In this extract, the Creature has just seen the De Lacey family leaving the cottage for the last time. Starting with this extract, write about how Shelley presents the Creature's desire for revenge in the novel. Write about:

- how Shelley presents the Creature's desire for revenge in this extract
- how Shelley presents attitudes to revenge in the novel as a whole.

[30 marks]

In the extract, the Creature burns the cottage because the family left him. This shows the passion and power of his feelings (1). He feels sadness then rage and he wants to get revenge. Shelley presents the Creature as a Romantic person unable to control his passions. The Creature uses poetic words to describe the movement of the clouds, 'loitered', and 'like a mighty avalanche' (2). Mary Shelley knew Romantic poets and Byron and Shelley were her friends (3). Shelley uses symbols that she uses elsewhere in the book – flames and darkness. Here we see the Creature's violent nature.

The extract shows how the Creature turned to revenge. He later says, 'if I cannot inspire love, I will cause fear' (4). The murders of William, Clerval and Elizabeth are all designed to make Victor feel as miserable and isolated as the Creature feels. The extract explains how he made a deliberate decision to pursue revenge because he could not find love or happiness in human society.

Violent revenge is a theme of the novel but only the Creature achieves it. It links the Creature and Victor, who also swears revenge saying that it is 'the devouring and only passion of my soul' (5) but for a long time he does not act. Only when he can't get legal help does he decide to pursue the Creature intending to kill him. However, the Creature continues to make Victor's life a misery. Revenge and bloody violence are themes in Gothic stories, which were popular in Shelley's time (6).

The extract is a turning point in the Creature's story. After this, he murders William, frames Justine, murders Henry and then Elizabeth. These are themes used by Gothic writers, who intended to shock and terrify readers (7). His violence would also have reminded readers of the time of the Reign of Terror, when mass executions took place during the French Revolution (8).

Shelley asks us to consider complex questions about revenge. Is it ever justified? Is the Creature justified in his desire for revenge, considering he was born only to be miserable? She presents the Creature sympathetically in places – someone born sensitive and human on the inside, but hideous to look at (9). Shelley also explores attitudes to revenge in Justine's trial and hanging, which is an example of flawed criminal justice. The death penalty is also a kind of legalised 'revenge'.

The Creature points out the hypocrisy of human 'justice' when he says, 'Am I to be thought the only criminal when all mankind sinned against me?' (10).

In the end, Victor and the Creature remain in a battle for revenge and only Victor's death ends it. The Creature's revenge is to taunt and lead Victor on and on, but Victor only wants to kill the Creature (11).

1. The first paragraph clearly states where the extract comes from in the novel. AO1

2. Detailed analysis of use of language but terminology not used. AO2

3. Reference to context but not linked to extract. AO3

4. Embedded quotation analysed, showing knowledge of the novel as a whole. AO1/AO2

5. Embedded quotation used effectively. AO1/AO2

6. Reference to literary context used to explain Shelley's choice of theme. AO3

7. Link to literary context but not analysed in reference to the theme. AO3

8. Reference to historical context but does not clearly exemplify the point. AO3

9. Shows knowledge of novel as a whole. AO1

10. Embedded quotation used but not analysed effectively. AO1

11. Conclusion does not contain a developed point. Could be developed further. AO1

Questions

EXAM PRACTICE

Choose a paragraph from this essay. Read it through a few times and then try to rewrite it and improve it. You might:

- Replace a reference with a quotation or use a better quotation.
- Ensure quotations are embedded in the sentence.
- Provide more detailed, or a wider range of, analysis.
- Use more subject terminology.
- Link some context to the analysis more effectively.

Grade 7+ Annotated Response

A proportion of the best top-band answers will be awarded Grade 8 or Grade 9. To achieve this, you should aim for a sophisticated, fluid and nuanced response that displays flair and originality.

Read the extract from Chapter 16 that begins 'I continued for the remainder' and ends 'reason and reflection' and then answer the question that follows.

In this extract, the Creature has just seen the De Lacey family leaving the cottage for the last time. Starting with this extract, write about how Shelley presents the Creature's desire for revenge in the novel. Write about:

- how Shelley presents the Creature's desire for revenge in this extract
- how Shelley presents attitudes to revenge in the novel as a whole.

[30 marks]

This extract tells how the Creature takes revenge on the cottagers for rejecting him. It also shows the passion and power of his feelings and how his actions are ruled by them (1). He feels sadness then rage and this fuels his desire for violent revenge. Shelley presents the Creature here as a Romantic soul tortured by misery and unable to control his passions. She gives the Creature a poetic voice, using personification to describe the movement of the clouds, 'loitered', and a natural simile 'like a mighty avalanche' (2), which is similar to the language used by Romantic poets such as Byron and Shelley – both were friends of Mary Shelley (3). Shelley uses the motifs of flames and darkness to create an atmosphere of malevolent mystery – motifs that she used when Victor performed his experiment. Here we see the Creature's violent nature.

The extract also shows the Creature turned to revenge after this part of the novel. The murders of William, Clerval and Elizabeth are all designed to make Victor feel as miserable and isolated as the Creature feels. The extract explains how he made a deliberate decision to pursue revenge because he could not find love or happiness in human society. He later says, 'if I cannot inspire love, I will cause fear', which implies that he decides to embrace the fate handed to him (4).

Violent revenge is a theme of the novel, and in this regard Shelley is drawing on the tradition of Gothic literature, which was popular at that time (5). Revenge links the Creature and Victor, who also swears revenge saying that it is 'the devouring and only passion of my soul' (6) but for a long time Victor does not act. Only when he can't get legal help does he decide to pursue the Creature intending to kill him. However, the Creature continues to make Victor's life a misery.

The extract is a turning point in the Creature's story. After this, he is committed to revenge and murders William, frames Justine, murders Henry and then Elizabeth (7). These acts are shocking, showing that Shelley was using themes used by Gothic writers, who intended to shock and terrify readers. His violence would also have reminded readers of the unleashed violence of the Reign of Terror, when mass executions took place during the French Revolution. This lawlessness was terrifying to educated society in other European countries (8), and viewed as a threat.

Shelley asks us to consider complex questions about revenge. Is it ever justified? Is the Creature justified in his desire for revenge, considering he was born only to be miserable? She presents the Creature sympathetically in places – someone born sensitive and human on the inside, but hideous to look at (9). Shelley explores attitudes to revenge in Justine's trial and hanging, which is an example of flawed criminal justice. The death penalty is also a kind of legalised 'revenge'. The Creature points out the hypocrisy of human 'justice' when he says, 'Am I to be thought the only criminal when all mankind sinned against me?' (10). Readers might sympathise with his point of view, but not his bloodthirsty quest for revenge.

1. The first paragraph clearly states where the extract comes from in the novel. AO1
2. Detailed analysis of use of language and terminology used. AO2
3. Reference to context linked to the extract. AO3
4. Embedded quotation analysed, showing knowledge of the novel as a whole. AO1/AO2
5. Reference to literary context used to explain Shelley's choice of theme. AO3
6. Embedded quotation used effectively. AO1/AO2
7. Broadens extract themes to relate to novel as a whole. AO1
8. Reference to historical context explains Shelley's presentation of theme. AO3
9. Shows knowledge of the novel as a whole. AO1
10. Embedded quotation used and analysed effectively. AO1

Questions

EXAM PRACTICE

Spend 45 minutes writing an answer to the following question.

Plan a response to the following exam question:

Read the extract from Chapter 4 that begins 'Two years passed' and ends 'at the university' and then answer the question that follows.

In this extract, Victor recalls his days as a student at Ingolstadt University. Starting with this extract, write about how Shelley presents attitudes to scientific discovery in the novel. Write about:

• how Shelley presents Victor's attitude to scientific discovery in this extract
• how Shelley presents attitudes to scientific discovery in the novel as a whole.

[30 marks]

Remember to use the plan you have already prepared.

Planning a Question Response

You must be able to: understand what an exam question is asking you and prepare a response.

How might an exam question be phrased?

A typical question will read like this:

Read the extract from Chapter 17 that begins 'How inconstant are your feelings!' and ends 'scope for your revenge' and then answer the question that follows.

In this extract, the Creature explains why Victor should create a companion for him. Starting with this extract, write about how Shelley presents the relationship between Victor and the Creature. Write about:

- how Shelley presents the relationship between Victor and the Creature in this extract
- how Shelley presents the relationship between Victor and the Creature in the novel as a whole.

[30 marks]

How do I work out what to do?

For AO1, you need to show a clear understanding of the characters of Victor and the Creature and the relationship between them.

For AO2, 'how' makes it clear you need to analyse the different ways Shelley's use of language and structure help to explore the relationship. You should analyse the extract and include quotations you have learned in your answer.

You also need to link your answer to the context of the novel to achieve your AO3 marks.

How can I plan my essay?

You have approximately 45 minutes to write your essay.

This isn't long but you should spend the first 5 minutes writing a quick plan. This will help you to focus your thoughts and write a well-structured essay.

Try to come up with five or six ideas. Each of these ideas can then be written up as a paragraph in the essay.

You can plan in whatever way you find most useful. Some students like to just make a quick list of points and then renumber them into a logical order. Spider diagrams are particularly popular; look at the example on the opposite page.

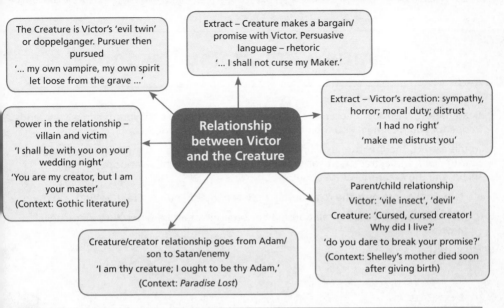

The Creature is Victor's 'evil twin' or doppelganger. Pursuer then pursued
'... my own vampire, my own spirit let loose from the grave ...'

Extract – Creature makes a bargain/promise with Victor. Persuasive language – rhetoric
'... I shall not curse my Maker.'

Relationship between Victor and the Creature

Extract – Victor's reaction: sympathy, horror; moral duty; distrust
'I had no right'
'make me distrust you'

Power in the relationship – villain and victim
'I shall be with you on your wedding night'
'You are my creator, but I am your master'
(Context: Gothic literature)

Parent/child relationship
Victor: 'vile insect', 'devil'
Creature: 'Cursed, cursed creator! Why did I live?'
'do you dare to break your promise?'
(Context: Shelley's mother died soon after giving birth)

Creature/creator relationship goes from Adam/son to Satan/enemy
'I am thy creature; I ought to be thy Adam,'
(Context: Paradise Lost)

 ## Summary

- Make sure you read the extract and the question carefully so that you know what the focus is.
- Remember to analyse how ideas are conveyed by Shelley.
- Try to relate your ideas to the novel's social and historical context.

 ## Questions

QUICK TEST

1. What key skills do you need to show in your answer?
2. What are the benefits of writing a quick plan for your essay?
3. Why is it important to read the extract carefully?

EXAM PRACTICE

Plan a response to the following exam question:

Read the extract from Chapter 10 that begins 'Believe me, Frankenstein' and ends 'work of your hands' and then answer the question that follows.

In this extract, the Creature entreats Victor to listen to his story. Starting with this extract, write about how Shelley presents the Creature in the novel. Write about:

- how Shelley presents the character of the Creature as sympathetic in this extract
- how Shelley presents the character of the Creature in the novel as a whole.

[30 marks]

Grade 5 Annotated Response

Read the extract from Chapter 17 that begins 'How inconstant are your feelings!' and ends 'scope for your revenge' and then answer the question that follows.

In this extract, the Creature explains why Victor should create a companion for him. Starting with this extract, write about how Shelley presents the relationship between Victor and the Creature. Write about:

- how Shelley presents the relationship between Victor and the Creature in this extract
- how Shelley presents the relationship between Victor and the Creature in the novel as a whole.

[30 marks]

In the extract, the Creature asks Victor for help and promises to disappear if Victor will make him a mate (1). When he says, 'I shall not curse my Maker' he is actually threatening Victor. The possessive adjective 'my' and the word 'Maker' remind Victor of his wrongdoing and his moral responsibility (2). He is really saying there will be consequences if Victor doesn't agree.

The extract shows Victor's response to the Creature's request. Briefly he feels sympathy, then remembers his moral duty but he is disgusted by the Creature, and he can't trust him (3). To Victor, this is just another way for the Creature to get revenge on him.

Shelley shows that Victor and the Creature can never have a healthy or loving parent-child relationship. Instead of being the Creature's protector and guide, Victor rejects the role. Victor curses him, calling him 'vile insect' and 'devil'. The Creature craves acceptance by Victor and society but he is spurned. We know that Shelley's mother died soon after she was born (4). When they meet, Victor is the one who behaves like a stroppy teenager, hurling insults while the Creature's language is more logical.

Shelley presents Victor and the Creature as creator and creature, but the power in the relationship is reversed: the Creature has power over his creator. She uses references to the epic poem Paradise Lost to indicate a change in the Creature's perception of his relationship to Victor (5). First, he thinks he is Victor's (God's) Adam, or beloved son – 'I ought to be thy Adam' (6). Then he compares himself to Satan, who was cast out of Paradise by God. The Creature then turns on his creator and vows revenge, like Satan. He still refers to Victor as 'Maker' and 'Creator' to remind Victor that they are forever linked, even though Victor hates him.

In the extract, the Creature cleverly makes Victor feel like he holds the power. He says to Victor, 'Make me happy and I shall again be virtuous' (7). However, we know that in this relationship the Creature holds power over Victor. When the Creature threatens, 'I shall be with you on your wedding night' after Victor has broken his promise, Victor knows he will act, and is frightened (8). He also tells Victor 'You are my creator, but I am your master'. This shows he knows he has the upper hand. Shelley uses the idea of passive victim (Victor) and threatening villain (the Creature), which was common in the Gothic fiction popular at the time (9).

Victor and the Creature are like two parts of the same person but their relationship is based on fear and mistrust. They never make peace with each other, even when Victor dies (10).

1. The first paragraph locates the extract in the context of the novel. AO1
2. Reference to themes in the extract supported by close textual analysis using terminology. AO1/AO2
3. Some analysis of theme but no close analysis of language in the extract. AO1
4. Reference to context but does not link to the point. AO3
5. Literary context is reference, linking to the novel. AO3
6. Effective use of quotation to exemplify a point. AO2
7. Embedded quotation used. AO1
8. Shows knowledge of the novel as a whole. AO1
9. Literary context used to exemplify a point. AO3
10. Conclusion is abrupt and the point is not developed. AO1

Questions

EXAM PRACTICE

Choose a paragraph from this essay. Read it through a few times and then try to rewrite it and improve it. You might:
- Replace a reference with a quotation or use a better quotation.
- Ensure quotations are embedded in the sentence.
- Provide more detailed, or a wider range of, analysis.
- Use more subject terminology.
- Link some context to the analysis more effectively.

Grade 7+ Annotated Response

A proportion of the best top-band answers will be awarded Grade 8 or Grade 9. To achieve this, you should aim for a sophisticated, fluid and nuanced response that displays flair and originality.

Read the extract from Chapter 17 that begins 'How inconstant are your feelings!' and ends 'scope for your revenge' and then answer the question that follows.

In this extract, the Creature explains why Victor should create a companion for him. Starting with this extract, write about how Shelley presents the relationship between Victor and the Creature. Write about:

- how Shelley presents the relationship between Victor and the Creature in this extract
- how Shelley presents the relationship between Victor and the Creature in the novel as a whole.

[30 marks]

In the extract, the Creature asks Victor for help and promises to disappear if Victor will make him a mate (1). His request links to Victor's original ambition to create 'a new species', which went badly wrong (2). When he says, 'I shall not curse my Maker' he is actually threatening Victor. The possessive adjective 'my' and the word 'Maker' remind Victor of his wrongdoing and his moral responsibility (3). He is really saying there will be consequences if Victor doesn't agree.

The extract shows Victor's response to the Creature's request. Briefly he feels sympathy, then remembers his moral duty (he thinks to himself 'I had no right'), but he is disgusted by the Creature, and he can't trust him (his words 'make me distrust you' show this) (4). To Victor, this is just another way for the Creature to get revenge on him.

Shelley shows that Victor and the Creature can never have a healthy or loving parent-child relationship. Instead of being the Creature's protector and guide, Victor rejects the role. Victor curses him, calling him 'vile insect' and 'devil'. The Creature craves acceptance by Victor and society but he is spurned. We know that Shelley's mother died soon after she was born so she knew what it feels like to be motherless and this may explain why we feel sympathy for the Creature even when he commits evil (5). When they meet, Victor is the one who hurls insults, while the Creature's language is more logical.

Shelley presents Victor and the Creature as creator and creature, but the power in the relationship is reversed: the Creature has power over his creator. She uses references to the epic poem Paradise Lost to indicate a change in the Creature's perception of his relationship to Victor (6). First, he thinks he is Victor's (God's) Adam, or beloved son – 'I ought to be thy Adam'. By using 'ought to' he reproaches Victor for rejecting him (7). Then he compares himself to Satan, who was cast out of Paradise by God. The Creature then turns on his creator and vows revenge, like Satan. He still refers to Victor as 'Maker' and 'Creator' to remind Victor that they are forever linked, even though Victor hates him.

In the extract, the Creature cleverly makes Victor feel like he holds the power. He says to Victor, 'Make me happy and I shall again be virtuous' (8). However, we know that in this relationship the Creature holds power over Victor. When the Creature threatens, 'I shall be with you on your wedding night' after Victor has broken his promise, Victor knows he will act, and is frightened (9). He also tells Victor 'You are my creator, but I am your master'. This shows he knows he has the upper hand. Shelley uses the idea of passive victim (Victor) and threatening villain (the Creature), which was common in the Gothic fiction popular at the time. Victor's horror and terror in response to the Creature makes him powerless and unable to act (10).

Victor and the Creature are linked from the moment of the Creature's birth. He shadows Victor like an evil twin. Shelley uses the literary device of 'doppelganger' to show that the Creature is like the worst part of Victor's character (11). Victor says he is like 'my own vampire, my own spirit let loose from the grave' – a continual reminder of Victor's failed ambition and moral weakness.

1. The first paragraph locates the extract in the context of the novel. AO1
2. Shows knowledge of novel as a whole. AO1
3. Some analysis of use of language and subject terminology used. AO2/AO1
4. Reference to themes in the extract supported by close textual analysis. AO1/AO2
5. Uses context to develop explanation of Shelley's presentation. AO3
6. Literary context is referenced, linking to the novel. AO3
7. Effective use of quotation to exemplify a point and language analysed. AO2
8. Embedded quotation used. AO1
9. Shows knowledge of the novel as a whole. AO1
10. Literary context used to exemplify a point and link to novel as a whole. AO3
11. Conclusion develops an idea, an embedded quote and analysis. AO1/AO2

Questions

EXAM PRACTICE

Spend 45 minutes writing an answer to the following question.

Plan a response to the following exam question:

Read the extract from Chapter 10 that begins 'Believe me, Frankenstein' and ends 'work of your hands' and then answer the question that follows.

In this extract, the Creature entreats Victor to listen to his story. Starting with this extract, write about how Shelley presents the Creature in the novel. Write about:

- how Shelley presents the character of the Creature as sympathetic in this extract
- how Shelley presents the character of the Creature in the novel as a whole.

[30 marks]

Remember to use the plan you have already prepared.

Glossary

Adjective – a word that describes a noun.

Banshee – a female spirit who cries out loudly to warn that someone is going to die

Bastille – it was the main prison in Paris and held political prisoners.

Biblical – relating to the Bible.

Confession – a statement confessing guilt or sin.

Creation story – a symbolic story of how the world began and how people came to inhabit it.

Doppelganger – a ghostly counterpart or double of a living person.

Enlightenment – an intellectual movement that emphasised reason and science rather than tradition.

Epic poem – a long narrative poem about significant heroic actions and events.

Exclamation – a word or sentence that expresses strong emotion.

Fatal flaw – a character deficiency that prevents a tragic hero from succeeding.

Feminist – a person who supports the rights of women.

Foil – a character who contrasts with another character in order to highlight that character's qualities.

French Revolution – an uprising in France (1789–1799) against the monarchy that resulted in the establishment of the French republic.

Galvanism – In biology, galvanism is the contraction of a muscle that is stimulated by an electric current.

Gothic fiction – a style of writing characterised by elements of terror, horror, death and the supernatural, as well as nature and very high emotion.

Grandiose – extravagant and imposing in style.

Hero – someone with admirable personal qualities who shows courage, virtue and resilience.

Hierarchy – a system of ranking according to status or importance.

Humanist – someone who does not follow a religion or believe in god. A Humanist believes that people can live ethical and fulfilling lives on the basis of reason and humanity.

Hypocrisy – claiming to have better standards or behaviour than is true.

Imagery – words used to create a picture in the imagination.

Imperative – a word or sentence that is a command.

Irony – something that seems the opposite of what was expected; deliberately using words that are the opposite of what was intended.

Latinate – derived from Latin.

Monosyllabic – words containing only one syllable.

Morality – a sense of right and wrong.

Myth – a traditional story, often symbolic in meaning.

Philosophy – a way of thinking about the world and society.

Populist – representing the interests of ordinary people.

Possessive adjective – an adjective used to show ownership.

Preface – the introductory statement to a written text.

Prometheus – in Greek mythology, a Titan who gave humans the gift of fire and was punished by Zeus.

Pronoun – a word that stands in place of a noun (such as: I, she, them, it).

Radical – new and different from what is traditional and known.

Rational – an attitude and way of thinking based on reason or logic.

Reign of Terror – a period (1793–1794) of the French Revolution characterised by a wave of executions of presumed enemies of the state.

Republic – a state in which power is held by the people's elected representatives and there is no monarch.

Rhetoric – language designed to have a persuasive or impressive effect.

Rhetorical question – a question asked for dramatic effect rather than to get an answer.

The Rime of the Ancient Mariner – a narrative poem by Samuel Taylor Coleridge published in 1798 in 'Lyrical Ballads', a collection of poems that essentially launched the Romantic movement in British poetry.

Romantic movement (Romanticism) – a movement in the late eighteenth and early nineteenth centuries in literature, music and art that celebrated imagination and nature rather than civilisation.

Sarcastic – using irony in order to mock or criticise.

Sinned – to have committed an immoral act.

Simile – a descriptive technique that compares one thing to another thing using 'like' or 'as'.

Sublime (literary) – a term used by Romantic artists to describe an experience of transcendence and awe in humans, generated by the power and majesty of nature.

Supernatural – a thing, being or event that defies logical or scientific understanding and the laws of nature.

Symbol – an object, colour, person or thing that represents a specific idea or meaning.

Tragic hero – a character who makes an error of judgement that leads to destruction.

Verb – a doing, feeling, thinking or being word.

Answers

Pages 4–5
Quick Test
1. St Petersburg.
2. His sister Margaret.
3. A gigantic figure on a sledge being pulled by dogs.
4. He nurses him back to health.
5. He hopes that Walton will learn a lesson from it.

Exam Practice

Answers might focus on how Shelley establishes Walton's character as a loner with hopes of glory, his isolated situation, the unexplained figure he sees and the fact that he finds the stranger compelling so that he wants to hear his story.

Analysis could include the effect of the adjective Walton uses – 'gigantic', which creates a sense of strangeness and that Walton is established as an ordinary man. The adjectives 'strange and harrowing' show that his interest and curiosity are aroused.

Pages 6–7
Quick Test
1. Elizabeth and William.
2. Henry Clerval.
3. His mother dies; he goes to university.
4. His own ego.
5. To collect body parts.

Exam Practice

Answers could centre on Victor's early experience of the power of electricity when he witnessed the storm and his mother's death, which made him want to have the power to bring the dead back to life using science.

Analysis might explore Victor's tone of voice as he is both proud of his achievement yet ashamed of how he achieved it. His use of the **verb** 'pursue' puts him in the role of aggressor or hunter and he personifies nature as female, as did the Romantic poets.

Pages 8–9
Quick Test
1. He is horrified by its appearance.
2. He recalls that night and the monster he created.
3. He is murdered.
4. Two years.
5. He suspects the Creature that he created murdered William and he knows that Justine is innocent.

Exam Practice

Comments might explore Victor's state of mind in rejecting the Creature – his horror and his need to escape, followed by a long illness prompted by a nervous reaction and guilt at what he has done.

Analysis might include Victor's use of exclamations to convey the strength of his emotions and use of strong, dramatic language: 'monster' to describe the Creature, which dehumanises him, and 'hell' showing that he associates the Creature with evil.

Pages 10–11
Quick Test
1. To feel better by seeing places he visited as a boy.
2. They were terrified and attacked him.
3. He saw his own reflection in a pool.
4. Beauty, gentleness, kindness and affection.
5. Family love and human affection.

Exam Practice

Answers might focus on the Creature's appreciation of natural beauty, his sensitivity to affection, his capacity for love and his horror at his own appearance.

Analysis could include the Creature's sophisticated vocabulary. His use of the word 'paradise' to describe his hovel has Biblical overtones and indicates that at this point he was in Eden. The adjective 'superior' shows that he prizes human society and considers himself inferior.

Pages 12–13
Quick Test
1. De Lacey.
2. By listening and observing Safie as she learns the language.
3. She secretly escaped from her father.
4. He burned down the cottage.
5. He wants Victor to create a female Creature.

Exam Practice

Answers could centre on the hurt that the Creature has suffered in being rejected by humans, and how he holds Victor responsible for creating him with so hideous an appearance that he can never be accepted.

Analysis might include the Creature's use of rhetorical questions and exclamations to express the dramatic passion of his feelings, his repetition of 'cursed/accursed' gives emphasis and use of Biblical language in the capitalised 'Creator' is calculated to remind Victor of their relationship.

Pages 14–15
Quick Test
1. He doesn't want to do it.
2. The Orkney Islands.
3. He sees the Creature at the window.
4. That he will be with Victor on his wedding night.
5. He is suspected of murder.

Exam Practice

Answers could talk about Victor agreeing because he has a moral sense of guilt at creating the Creature and a sense of responsibility, plus he is frightened of the Creature. He destroys the She-Creature in anger and to get revenge on the Creature but also because he knows it would be wrong to do it.

Analysis might explore Victor's use of 'filthy', meaning dirty and vile to show his disgust at the task. He has used the same word to describe the Creature – 'filthy mass'. His use of the words 'enthusiastic frenzy' to describe his experiment imply he believes he is more rational now than he was.

Pages 16–17

Quick Test

1. He was strangled.
2. The Creature.
3. The Creature's threat to be with him on his wedding night.
4. He is not believed.
5. He makes Victor endure terrible hardship and leaves him taunting messages.

Exam Practice

Comments could explore how their roles have been reversed with Victor now pursuing the Creature instead of the Creature shadowing Victor. Analysis might talk about the Creature's message 'my reign is not yet over' that is calculated to goad Victor into continuing, although he knows it is a hopeless quest. Yet, it is the only thing keeping him alive. The Creature's language is about power ('reign') while Victor still talks about 'hell', 'devil' and being 'cursed', words that emphasise his lack of power in the relationship at this point.

Pages 18–19

Quick Test

1. Walton has seen the Creature with his own eyes and he has seen Safie's letters to Felix.
2. To continue his pursuit of the Creature.
3. He is distraught.
4. First sympathy, then accuses him of hypocrisy.
5. Their desire for revenge.

Exam Practice

Answers could centre on the Creature's distress at Victor's death and his admiration for him, despite everything. The Creature also weeps for what he was forced to become – a 'malignant devil' but now it is over, he is looking forward to death as a release from misery.

Analysis might explore how the Creature uses language that Victor used to refer to him – 'devil'. He uses grandiose exclamations to convey the force of his grief 'Oh Frankenstein!' and archaic **pronoun** and verb forms 'thou wert', which add significance and weight to his meaning.

Pages 20–21

Quick Test

1. Narrative framing of three first-person narratives.
2. It establishes credibility and rationality.
3. It creates a sense of distance, so that the Creature's narrative takes on a mythological tone.
4. It makes readers believe the story must have happened.

Exam Practice

Answers could mention how the narrative frames enable the reader to understand the whole story, which can't be told by only one narrator. How the technique and shifts back in time create a sense of distance for the reader, giving the Creature's narrative an almost mythological quality. They might also mention the timeline that loops back from the present day to the past and back again in a symmetrical pattern.

Analysis might include how Victor and the Creature use persuasion and **imperatives** ('remember', 'hear') to get and hold their listener's attention. Each feels an urgent need to explain, or confess, their actions.

Pages 22–23

Quick Test

1. She died.
2. She was used to discussing philosophy and ideas of the day.
3. In Switzerland.
4. Who could tell the scariest story.

Exam Practice

Answers could mention how Shelley's unconventional education and exposure to radical thinking made her unafraid to explore the shocking themes in *Frankenstein*. Comments might include how Shelley's motherless upbringing led her to explore themes of birth and death and make links between the effect that Victor's mother's death has on him, and that the Creature is motherless.

Pages 24–25

Quick Test

1. The ordinary people.
2. A period of mass executions during the French Revolution.
3. The Creature.
4. That revenge and violence solve nothing.

Exam Practice

Answers might explore how the Creature is not constrained by human law and responds with violence to what he considers to be injustice. Analysis might focus on Victor's use of the word 'horror' to describe the Creature's actions – civilised society had the same reaction to the actions of the mob during the French Revolution.

Pages 26–27

Quick Test

1. The ideas of the Enlightenment.
2. That it is essentially unknowable, mysterious and that man should not try to control it.
3. He is a scientist who thinks he can control nature.
4. He is sensitive to the power and beauty of nature.

Exam Practice

Answers might consider how Victor and the Creature respond to nature in a Romantic, sometimes poetic, way as an uplifting force for good. Comments might include how in the pursuit of his scientific ambitions, Victor isolates himself from society and his act of creating life from death contravenes nature's law.

Pages 28–29

Quick Test

1. To entertain readers by exciting their emotions and feelings.
2. Female readers.
3. It was intended to terrify and enthral its readers.

Exam Practice

Answers could talk about the following Gothic elements that feature in *Frankenstein*: violent death (the Creature's murders); fear of the unknown (Victor's fear of the Creature); nightmares (Victor's mental state); darkness (when the Creature is brought to life); unexplained and unnatural events

Answers 77

Answers

(the mystery surrounding Victor's act of creation). Analysis could focus on the graphic and horrifying description of Elizabeth's corpse, 'bloodless' and 'relaxed' like a doll and Victor's frequent use of the word 'horror' to describe his feelings.

Pages 30–31
Quick Test
1. In the Preface.
2. In his thirst for forbidden knowledge and his ambition to know and control the source of life.
3. Because, like Adam, he was brought to life from no person.

Exam Practice

Answers might focus on how both Victor and the Creature can fill different roles in the creation story – Victor tries to be God but is more like Satan, and the Creature was born to be an Adam but instead resembled Satan. Analysis might include the Creature's use of Biblical **imagery** ('creator', 'maker') and archaic forms 'thou', 'wert' drawn from *Paradise Lost*, which is echoed by Victor's use of 'devil' and 'fiend' to refer to the Creature, and 'cherub' and 'celestial' to refer to Elizabeth.

Pages 32–33
Quick Test
1. So that we learn of events and characters through him.
2. That he is a noble soul brought low by misery.
3. He falls ill or finds ways to distract himself.
4. He is horrified at the Creature's hideous appearance.

Exam Practice

Comments might consider how Victor presents himself as a tragic hero turned victim due to fate. He says his ambition drove him to fulfil a great purpose in life like a hero but, ironically, this is what turns him into a victim of the Creature's relentless desire for revenge.

Pages 34–35
Quick Test
1. He is bigger, more powerful and moves faster than an ordinary man.
2. He is attacked and rejected.
3. In revenge for the cottagers' treatment of him.
4. He weeps.

Exam Practice

Answers might consider how the Creature blames Victor for creating him with a hideous appearance but the capacity to feel and appreciate love and beauty, thus condemning him to a life of misery: yet he feels regret when Victor dies. Analysis could mention how the Creature refers to Victor as 'creator' and 'maker', a continual reminder of their relationship and of Victor's responsibility, and how he tries to manipulate Victor, alternately pleading for sympathy then making threats.

Pages 36–37
Quick Test
1. His noble nature.
2. To achieve glory.
3. At the end of the novel.
4. He accepts he has failed in his mission.

Exam Practice

Answers might focus on their dreams of personal glory, failed ambitions, their single-minded pursuit of an enterprise, sense of destiny and their interest in scientific discovery. Analysis might explore how Walton's grandiose, heroic language sets the tone for Victor's narrative. Both talk of 'fate' and 'destiny' and think they have a 'great purpose' to fulfil.

Pages 38–39
Quick Test
1. He meets Victor the morning after he has brought the Creature to life.
2. Sanity, normality, good humour and virtue.
3. His interests are romantic and imaginative compared with Victor's interest in science.
4. He strangles him.

Exam Practice

Answers could explore how the privileges that Henry enjoyed (a loving family and friends, a good education) were denied to the Creature. Henry is integrated in society and he is happy. The Creature is excluded and expresses his resentment through violence. Analysis might comment on Victor's use of 'formed' in his description of Henry, the same verb he uses for the Creature 'the wretch … I had endeavoured to form', unconsciously contrasting Henry's worth with the Creature's lack of it.

Pages 40–41
Quick Test
1. He idealises her as a symbol of goodness and beauty.
2. He travels to Ireland to speak on his son's behalf at the trial.
3. To university.
4. She is hanged.

Exam Practice

Answers might consider how Shelley uses these characters to draw a moral contrast with the behaviour and motivation of the main characters, Victor and the Creature. Therefore, they do not need to be much more than symbolic. Analysis might consider that Victor's use of absolute terms, 'cherub' and 'celestial', shows his extreme personality. He tends to see things as black or white.

Pages 42–43
Quick Test
1. Human society, values, communication and the power of family affection.
2. They have been exiled from their native country, France.
3. They are the only family he has known.
4. He learns language.

Exam Practice

Answers could mention that the De Laceys make the Creature realise how hopeless his situation is and his experience with them pushes him towards a path of evil and vengeance on mankind. Analysis might consider how the Creature uses idealised language to describe them, similar to that which Victor uses about his family. The hovel is 'paradise', the family is 'superior' and Safie is 'angelic'.

Pages 44–45

Quick Test

1. Justine Moritz and Victor Frankenstein.
2. 'wretched mockery of justice'.
3. Take justice into their own hands.

Exam Practice

Answers could explore examples of justice – Justine's punishment, Victor's punishment by the Creature and the Creature's punishment by 'all human kind'. Analysis might include Victor's disgust at the 'wretched mockery' of Justine's trial, his sense that the Creature's request is just, given his situation, and the Creature's view that his criminality is justified given society's treatment of him.

Pages 46–47

Quick Test

1. Romantic writers.
2. Personification.
3. Sublime.
4. As a Romantic.

Exam Practice

Ideas might include how nature's power is linked to human emotions, such as the electrical storm that showed Victor the power of nature and began his obsession with creating life. Analysis might include how his use of the word 'sublime' to show his sense of nature's uplifting power (in the Alps), the Creature's exclamations, showing his spirits uplifting in spring, and how Shelley's presentation of nature takes on a symbolic value when Victor chases the Creature through the Arctic.

Pages 48–49

Quick Test

1. Robert Walton and Victor Frankenstein.
2. Galvanism.
3. He witnesses electricity destroying a tree during a thunderstorm.

Exam Practice

Answers could compare and contrast the aims and outcomes of Walton's expedition and Victor's experiment. Walton is like Victor at an earlier stage of development. Victor intends his story to be a lesson to Walton. Analysis might consider how they use the same phrase 'acquirement of knowledge', but for Victor, it is 'dangerous', while for Walton, it is his goal.

Pages 50–51

Quick Test

1. As a close and loving one.
2. Protectors.
3. Whenever he wants to perform an experiment.

Exam Practice

Answers could explore the following: the Creature's happiness when he is close to the De Laceys; his desire to be accepted by them; his other attempts to approach humans; Walton's need for a close friend; Victor's love for his parents and Elizabeth, as well as his close friendship with Clerval. Analysis might consider how the Creature's use of 'protectors' shows that he feels almost as if the De Laceys have adopted him – they are his 'link' to society. His question to Victor shows how keenly he feels the lack of parental love.

Pages 52–53

Quick Test

1. Gloomy and mysterious.
2. He faints.
3. When he returns to the laboratory.
4. They are passive victims, placed in dangerous situations.

Exam Practice

Answers might focus on the following: the creation of the Creature; how Shelley uses light and dark imagery to create an atmosphere of mystery and foreboding; how colours and textures create a repulsive description of him; how Victor reacts with terror and horror. Analysis could focus on Victor's use of the word 'horror' (he often uses it to describe his reaction to the Creature), 'unhallowed' meaning unholy or wicked and 'grave' creating a sense of something unnatural and evil, as well as 'tremble' and 'swim' to show that his reaction is physical as well as psychological, like a Gothic heroine, it seems he is about to faint.

Pages 54–55

Quick Test

1. He is a noble soul brought low by destiny or fate.
2. *A Modern Prometheus*.
3. Showing courage in the face of adversity.

Exam Practice

Answers could explore how far Victor really is a tragic hero and how far he brought his destiny upon himself with his experiment and whether the Creature is a tragic hero as he could not control his destiny – although he thought he could. Doomed to be miserable, his actions failed to change its course. Analysis might comment on Victor's sense that he is powerless to change his destiny, in contrast to the Creature, who rejects 'slavery' and fights to control his destiny.

Pages 56–57

Quick Test

1. It debates the relative importance of innate qualities versus experience in guiding our behaviour.
2. He rejects his creation.
3. He never gets the chance to integrate into human society.

Exam Practice

Answers could explore how the Creature maintains until the end that by nature he was born 'benevolent and good' but that his experience of life forced him to embrace evil, seek vengeance and commit terrible crimes. Analysis might consider

Answers

how the Creature's higher-order vocabulary and language acquisition prove his intelligence and learning power; at the same time, the pile-up of verbs 'spurned/kicked/trampled on' shows his fury at the treatment he has received.

Pages 60–61
Practice Questions
Use the mark scheme below to self-assess your strengths and weaknesses. The estimated grade boundaries are included so you can assess your progress towards your target grade.

Pages 62–63
Quick Test
1. Understanding of the whole text, specific analysis and terminology, awareness of the relevance of context, a well-structured essay and accurate writing.
2. Planning focusses your thoughts and allows you to produce a well-structured essay.
3. Quotations give you more opportunities to do specific AO2 analysis.

Exam Practice
Ideas might include the following: Victor links scientific discovery with fulfilment of personal glory; we understand the strength of its attraction for him; he isolated himself in single-minded pursuit of it; this was the source of his downfall; the example of Walton as a fellow-discoverer and the Creature as the product of a scientific experiment; the uneasy relationship between science and nature.

Pages 66–67 and 72–73
Exam Practice
Use the mark scheme below to self-assess your strengths and weaknesses. Work up from the bottom, putting a tick by things you have fully accomplished, a ½ by skills that are in place but need securing and underlining areas that need particular development. The estimated grade boundaries are included so you can assess your progress towards your target grade.

Pages 68–69
Quick Test
1. Understanding of the whole text, specific analysis and terminology, awareness of the relevance of context, a well-structured essay and accurate writing.
2. Planning focusses your thoughts and allows you to produce a well-structured essay.
3. Quotations give you more opportunities to do specific AO2 analysis.

Exam Practice
Ideas might include the following: Contrast between how the Creature presents his innate nature as benevolent and his actions; how society's treatment moulded his character; strength of the Creature's powers of persuasion and use of rhetoric to influence Victor; his appeal to Victor's compassion and the link between them; his use of Biblical terms; his view of human justice and sense of injustice shown towards himself.

Grade	AO1 (12 marks)	AO2 (12 marks)	AO3 (6 marks)
6–7+	A convincing, well-structured essay that answers the question fully. Quotations and references are well-chosen and integrated into sentences. The response covers the whole novel.	Analysis of the full range of Shelley's methods. Thorough exploration of the effects of these methods. Accurate range of subject terminology.	Exploration is linked to specific aspects of the novel's contexts to show detailed understanding.
4–5	A clear essay that always focusses on the exam question. Quotations and references support ideas effectively. The response refers to different points in the novel.	Explanation of Shelley's different methods. Clear understanding of the effects of these methods. Accurate use of subject terminology.	References to relevant aspects of context show clear understanding.
2–3	The essay has some good ideas that are mostly relevant. Some quotations and references are used to support the ideas.	Identification of some different methods used by Shelley to convey meaning. Some subject terminology.	Some awareness of how ideas in the novel link to its context.